Edna Page   Nora Penfold.

BALDOCK VOICES

BALDOCK VOICES

The town as remembered by Baldock People in conversation with Edna Page and Nora Penfold

Foreword by Nigel Hawthorne

Edited by Maureen Maddren

EGON PUBLISHERS LTD

For Ron Page
who loved Baldock well

First published in 1991 by
Egon Publishers Ltd, Royston Road, Baldock, Herts SG7 6NW

Copyright © Egon Publishers Ltd

ISBN 0 905858 62 X

Designed by Nick Maddren
Campion Publishing Services, Baldock SG7 6DB
for Egon Publishers Ltd

Printed in England by
Streetsprinters, Royston Road, Baldock, Herts SG7 6NW

End papers: Crowds in the High Street waiting for the crowning of Baldock's Festival Queen, 1951.
Half-title: Schoolgirls, 1902.
Title spread: Celebrations for Edward VII's coronation, 1902.
Page 5: The 'Wotsanames' concert party.
Page 6: An outing in 'The Optimist'.
Page 8: Mrs Blaxall and Mrs Bray, residents of Wynn's Almshouses, 1925.

Contents

Acknowledgements

We should like to acknowledge the co-operation given to us by the following contributors, without whom this book would not have been possible.

The Baldock Society, the late Mr G Barker, Mr P Brand, Gary O'Brien, Mrs P Bye, the late Mrs A Bysouth, the late Mr F A Castle, Mr A Chapman, Mrs M Charter, Ada Clowes, Mr C Cooper, Mrs M Cooper, Mrs H Darts, Mrs E Eales, Mr and Mrs S Eales, Mrs D Edwards, Mrs E K Ellis, Mrs N Emery, Robert Eversden, Mr P Farr, Mr A W Flesch, Mrs M Gale, Mrs H Gray, Mrs P Green, Mrs C Guiver, Mr W Huckle, Mr R James, Mr and Mrs R Juffs, Mr and Mrs R Knight, Mr R Marshall, Jean Morris, Mrs M Olney, Edna Page, Mary Parry, Chris Penfold, Harry Penfold, Nora Penfold, Miss M Pooley, Mrs E Reddall, Derek Slaney, Linda Slaney, Mr and Mrs W Woods.

We are grateful to the following for their kind permission in allowing us to reproduce their photographs in this book. The Baldock Society: Jacket front, end papers, pp. 8, 12-13, 14, 15, 19, 20, 21, 23, 24, 30, 33, 44-5, 50, 53, 54, 62, 70, 71, 74, 75, 77, 79, 80, 82, 85, 91, 95 btm, 99, 111, 113 btm, 115 top, 116-7, 129 btm, 136-7, 150, 153, 157. Paul Castle: 14, 16, 17, 22, 25, 31, 32, 39, 41, 42 btm, 47, 49, 57, 59, 67, 69, 73, 76, 81, 86, 89, 95 top, 96, 98, 108-9, 113 top, 115 btm. Baldock Community Association, Baldock Mail, R Barker, W Beechener, G O'Brien, R Chapman, A Clarke, F Clarke, N Dilley, R Eversden, D Gentle, E Gray, J Gray, D Head, Hitchin Museum, D Hoeg, N Maddren, North Herts Gazette, P Newman, M Olney, E Page, R Page, M Parry, N Penfold, P Price, J S Rider, R Ridley, Mrs Schramli, A Stevenson, V L Townsend, E Trigg, R Wilkins, P Wilsher.

We should also like to thank everyone who provided us with photographs so that we were able to make a selection out of over 550 received.

Grateful thanks are also due to Elizabeth Eversden for her invaluable assistance in the preparation of this book.

While every effort has been made to credit the owners of all the illustrations and the originators of some of the information used in the book, we regret any omission that may have occurred.

Foreword

'I can remember what happened sixty years ago, but I couldn't tell you what happened yesterday.' I wonder how often one has heard that said?

One of Man's incalculable gifts is his ability to forget, erasing a cruel memory as though it had never happened, or have it slip away into the subconscious, as a ship vanishes into the fog, taking with it the painful reality. The image and the emotion each softening with the passage of time.

Another of his gifts is his ability to remember. Often in microscopic detail. The passing on of these memories can prove an extraordinary experience to those on the receiving end – if one recalls the Ancient Mariner – it can be poignant and it can be humorous. It can throw open a window onto the past, inviting us, the audience, to step back in time and piece together events as they were.

Such was my experience on reading 'Baldock Voices'. It's full of insight and daft, idiosyncratic perceptions.

Who could resist characters like 'Whirly Jellis' with his hearth balls of chalk loading his donkey cart to sell them round the town? Or that sharp truth 'People were often content, but on Monday, Tuesday, Wednesday and Thursday there wasn't much to eat, just bread and scrape.'

Then there was the legendary Totty Rayner – crossed in love, umbrella up, always in black. '. . . I remember hearing her speak one day up near the Station. She asked someone if they'd seen a grey-haired man . . .'

Also, the fellow who claimed to have made artificial pips for Tickler's raspberry jam – the book is full of these riches.

It's traditional, I suppose, to decry the present and say that nothing ever quite matches up to the past. But, it would be wonderful to think that, amidst all the hustle and bustle of this modern world, the little details, the simple things in life didn't slip by unnoticed.

It is this small collection of memories and anecdotes which transports us, the reader, so effortlessly back to a world where the pace, perhaps, was slower, but the characters more colourful, more eccentric than they are today. Or do they just seem so?

I'm certain of one thing. As a resident of Baldock and one who frequently takes the train up to London at Baldock Station, it will be difficult in the future to stand on the platform and not think of the territorials being waved off to France amongst all the flags and bunting and the hurray hurrays! – 'But half of 'em never came back....'

Nigel Hawthorne, C.B.E.

Introduction

History is composed of a series of well-documented events, but all too frequently the details of the lives of 'ordinary' people have been lost – people who were often untouched by those great national or political happenings that were later to be recorded in the history books. Wars, of course, affected everyone, but they brought their own problems to people on the 'home front' which were far removed and more fundamental than those concerning the politicians.

This book is an attempt to record and preserve the memories of people living in Baldock during the first seventy years of this century. Hours of taped conversations form the basis of the text and because the memories are in the actual words of the people themselves, past events have a vigorous quality that eliminates the time barrier, so that we feel we really know what the town was like thirty, fifty, even seventy years ago.

In this book we have been able to use only half of the material collected, but nevertheless every taped conversation has been used, at least in part. The remainder has been carefully filed away and will undoubtedly be utilised in some way in the future.

Although BALDOCK VOICES charts the changes in the town from approximately 1900 to 1970, it will not be a complete record of events – that was never the intention – but we hope that it gives a flavour of life in a small country town and shows how gradual, but dramatic, change has come about in a comparatively short space of time. Indeed, because of the rapid strides made by science, industry and technology, the 70 years covered by this book have witnessed the greatest changes ever seen in one person's lifetime.

We are grateful to all the people who agreed to have their memories recorded and to the many others who got in touch when the book was in preparation. Without their willing assistance, all the interesting minutiae of everyday life would have been lost. We are certain that this book will be a valuable resource in years to come not only for social historians but for anyone who wants to know what life was *really* like during the first half of the 20th century.

High St. Baldock.

The
Small Country Town
1900 to 1920s

Overleaf: Top end of the High Street c. 1910 with South Lodge in the distance and the large elms in the grounds of Elmwood Manor on the right.

Baldock in 1900 was a small country town of just over 2000 inhabitants. It wasn't a wealthy place, although there were a number of large houses whose owners each kept a considerable staff of servants. There were farms in the town and it wasn't unusual to meet cows in the street going to and from milking, or to one of the many slaughter-houses. The needs of everyday living were well-catered for by a variety of shops, and errand boys would deliver to the doorstep, if required. The town was virtually self-sufficient and, as many people remembered, in the summer it was a beautiful place to be, with large trees lining the High Street and plenty of leafy lanes to walk down on a Sunday evening. This, then, is the town in the years up to and including the First World War.

The High Street hasn't altered hardly a bit since the First World War. There were three cottages near William Sale's farm at the top end of the town; they've gone and there are flats there now. I knew nearly all the houses and occupants. I was a paperboy up that way. Dr Day lived in the Gates. My old dad worked on the brewery and he was a bit on the stout side and he weren't well so he goes over to old Dr Day – hooked-nosed man he was – and he went in and said, 'I'm a bit out of sorts, Doctor.' So the Doctor says, 'Well you know your trouble, don't you.' 'No I don't,' says me dad, 'or else I shouldn't have come.' So he says, 'Too much Simpsons that's your trouble.' (Dr Day was a teetotaller.) So Dad says, 'Well, if I didn't think you wasn't going to tell me anything else, I shouldn't have come.'

Veasey, the solicitor, lived in Pepper Court. At the White Lion there was a white lion laying on a platform at the front of the pub (on the roof) – a wooden one. There was a pub in Jackson Street, The Bushell and Strike. In those days we had no water laid on, no gas nor electric light. We used to go to bed with a candle, there was an oil lamp on the table and we had a pump in the yard that supplied the three cottages. We used to have to put a bucket of water down the toilet. Fortunately we were on the sewer which was a blessing in those days.

The town was lit by gas, there was a street lamp near where we played in Orchard Road and there was a man employed to go round and put the lamps on and then go round late at night to put them out. I got into trouble one night – my dad said, 'You've been teasing Mr Dilley.' You know what kids are - we used to call him 'cock'orny' and annoy him and he told his brother and his brother

The High Street c. 1900.

told me dad, so we had to stop that. He used to go round every night with a long pole and pull the chain and light the lamp.

There was a farm in Church Street (Waterloo Farm) – some people called Logsdon had it and every day the cows from the farm used to come up the twitchell up into Jackson Street, cross Jackson Street and up into Football Close. Then up into what we used to call the Turnpike and graze on the field up there – in between the Turnpike and the Royston Road – they grazed all day and came back at night.

One of the hobbies we had – we used to sit on the Great North Road with a bit of paper and a pencil taking car numbers and you might wait half-an-hour before one came along.

Butchers used to kill in the town – Coopers had a slaughter yard in what we used to call Brewery Yard. I believe it's called Brewery Lane now. Deans used to kill in the bottom of our road (Orchard Road) at a place at the back. Worbeys had a slaughterhouse up Pesthouse Lane near where the garage is, in a shed in a field. Five butchers we had and four or five bakers, and Mr Izzard used to do a bit of cooking in Pembroke Road. It was a nice little community.

There was a butcher's on the corner of Orchard Road kept by a lady called Mrs Nash who used to do a bit of dancing (professional dancing) and she taught Charlie Scoot who used to dance a bit at

A water-cart laying the dust in Church Street.

Church Street c. 1910. Waterloo Farm is the ivy-covered house on the right, near the telegraph pole.

the fair. And when she got older it changed hands and Wilkerson stepped in and they moved up the street to where Chapmans is, There was a slaughterhouse up Orchard Road and we often watched them drive one of Saville's old cows in there – it wasn't best quality meat.

Wilson's, 'The Noted Cheap Clothing House', Whitehorse Street, 1910.

Butchers did their own slaughtering in Baldock. Mr Cooper had a place in Brewery Yard. We'd sometimes help drive the cows in and we used to let one go now and again just for the fun of it and that used to run all around and we'd chase it, but the butcher didn't like them running around if they were about to slauther them 'cos it made them tough.

We had gas lamps in the town when I was a girl. An old man used to come round about ten o'clock and put them out. He'd light them when it got dusk. His name was Scales and he was in the Salvation Army so we used to get a little treat from him now and again! The Salvation Army used to meet in a hut in Football Close where the Garage is now. They would come round on a Sunday evening and stand under the lamp – quite strong they were. And there was a Primitive Methodist Chapel in Church Street and I remember a person name of Hyde being buried there and our teacher Mr Bennett picked a few of us to go and sing in the chapel at the funeral, 'Jesu, lover of my soul,' I think the hymn was. They used to have services there, old man named Smith from Norton came to preach on Sunday evenings – he was a farm labourer and he'd stand up there in the pulpit and preach 'til the sweat ran down his face.

There were farms in the town – New Farm, where Brandles Close now is – and Waterloo Farm, in Church Street, kept by

King Edward VII is cheered on his way home from Newmarket by, among others, maids leaning out of an upstairs window and an old soldier giving a salute.

Logsdons. If we had to go there and get a hap'orth of milk before we went to school we knew we were going to have milk pudding for dinner. Logsdons were church people. They kept cows there at the back and they would be taken to neighbouring fields during the day and brought back to be milked in the afternoon and, of course, wherever they went, there was a mess. You can see from the old photographs where the horses had been along the roads. The pavements were pebbled, they weren't smooth like they are now and the roads would be made up with flint at the beginning of the year and the steam roller would be there to press it down. If King Edward VII was coming through to go to Newmarket, they would let us out of school to line up, and I remember one particular afternoon we all lined up, then when we got back to school, Mr Bennett said, 'Well, hands up, who saw the King then?' and Stanley Bishop stood up and said, 'We couldn't see him for bloody dust, Sir,' which was true because of the state of the roads – so you can imagine what happened to him. He was a case he was – had that little place down Clacton. 'Come and see the lion' – well, of course, it was a dandelion and he had a snake there as well one year. He was in the army – in the Bedfords – he kicked his hat all the way down the street in Folkestone when they were going off on board ship.

Mr Ridley was the carrier and the old women would stand at the Cross on a Monday waiting with their husband's suits for him to come along and pawn them for them in Hitchin and then they'd wait on a Friday and he'd bring them back.

We had a very quiet life before the First World War. I still can't stand a lot of noise – I think it was better then. We lived in Sun Street and there was a shop next door – tinsmiths, ironmongers and so on – a Mr Thoroughgood and he used to go with a cart and horse round the villages. Opposite to us was a pub, The Saracen's Head and you entered it from the corner. The town looked beautiful in those days with all the big trees along the High Street.

There was Simpsons Brewery in the High Street and another down Church Street. Wells and Winch's at the back of where Mulberry Court now is. And when Letchworth was being built it was used as a hostel for the unemployed men who came down from London to work in Letchworth.

There are six very old cottages in South Road, where the draymen lived. To enable these men to get to work early, about 4.00 am in the morning, a man was employed by the Brewery called a knocker-up. He would call at the cottages at 3.00 am every morning. He had a long pole with a large solid ball at the top. He would knock on the two bricks near the small bedroom on each cottage, by doing so these bricks were badly defaced and were very prominent, until a few years ago when the cottages were modernised.

Whitehorse Street showing Butler's Garage, Farr's Bakers (with a blind covering the window) and Booth's Stores. The king drove along here on his way to the races at Newmarket, hence the large number of flagpoles.

A wedding party in the front garden of the house of the coachman to 'The Wilderness'. The large trees of Avenue Field are in the background.

The shops in Baldock really were shops then — you could go and look in the windows — and what was better than Booths, Bishops and Moss's – you'd go and sit in there and have a natter – 'How's your mother and how's your father?' – but now it's only your money they want. There was the lovely smell of ham and the lovely smell of coffee – ooh, glory be! Even if you hadn't got any money you could smell.

Ted Booth, one of the sons of Booths the draper's, was supposed to go to Southend to see his old landlady and stay with her for a fortnight's holiday – anyway he didn't come back. So they got in touch with her and found he'd never been there. They were in a panic, of course, 'Whatever had happened to Ted?' They got the police in and all sorts of things. He seemed to have disappeared off the face of the earth. A few days later they got a cablegram; 'I'm on my way to Canada, I'll write when I'm settled.' They were relieved when they knew. He went out there and became an ice cream vendor, a photographer on the beach, all sorts of things, then he came back to Baldock and worked for Horne Brothers.

Now the bakers — there was Barkers in Church Street just beyond The Star, it's an electrical shop now. We used to say 'Barker Baker Baldock bakes brown bread,' He had three sons and their mother was a governor of Pond Lane School.

Baldock was never a rich town, but there was money in it, of course; whether they spent their money in Baldock or not, I don't know, but there was Beldam's in the Park and the South Lodge people and the Veaseys and Captain Smith in the old surgery next to Days, and people in The Grange where the Goldcrest is now. People called Morris lived in the Wilderness and they used to have a lot of theatrical people there at weekends – Ellaline Terriss was one. I was friendly with the gardener's daughter and he had to get extra in to feed them so she'd tell us and we'd go to church on Sunday morning to see who was there and they dressed up a lot and had horses and carriages.

'The Wilderness', Hitchin Street, c. 1900. The photo also shows the avenue of trees in what was to become Avenue Park.

Gardeners in the greenhouse at 'The Wilderness'.

Sir Benjamin and Lady Cherry lived at the Grange and it was about Baldock Fair time that she was desperately ill, so straw was laid down the length of the street so that the wheels of the carts wouldn't clatter over the road and disturb her.

Baldock wasn't very wealthy until all the factories came to Letchworth. Nothing seemed to change when I was a lad – there were the well-off people and the not-so-well-off, right down to the ordinary people, so separated they were. And it was the same in the church – all the dignitaries were the well-off people – Mr William Sale and all that lot. A lot of them were maltsters – going back to the 17th century.

I was born and bred in Baldock, in Coleman's Court, backing onto 9 Hitchin Street. There used to be a passageway from Hitchin Street into the Court and there were five houses there. The house next door used to be the police station and the cell is still there – I was locked up in it one night for a punishment.

I was an errand boy and delivered 7lb packs of corn to the villages – Ashwell, Weston and so on. I got 10/– a week. Then I went apprenticed to Mr Raban in Sun Street and worked there until the war. He also had a glass-cutting shop. Jim Christmas had a general store in Church Street and Mrs Timms had another one in Church Street near The Bull's Head selling paraffin and oil. There used to be four houses between Mrs Timms' house and The Bull's Head and a little passageway between these houses and The Bull's Head leading to Barker's Yard. Then you came out of Barker's Yard – there were houses there, too, across a little right of way and into another yard called Payne's Yard. Mr Payne was a coalman – he lived in one of the three houses there.

At the back of the yard there was an orchard with a passageway behind where the Guide Hut now is. There used to be little cottages at the back of the churchyard, too, and there was a farm in Norton Road. We had a barber called Mr Hergert who used to pull teeth out.

You could get everything in the shops in those days – everything from a pin to a gent's suit. You could go in one end (of

Hitchin Street c. 1910 showing the police station, with its lamp over the door.

Baldock Cross c. 1900 with Hergert's barber's shop on the left, Buckingham's tobacconist's and The Plume of Feathers public house, which closed in 1902.

Booths) and buy everything you wanted and come out the other. Next door you could get complete outfits for ladies – shoes as well.

Baldock was a thriving town and the centre for all the villages around. It was a prosperous time with lots of big houses – they could get all the staff here – chauffeurs, servants, gardeners, housekeepers, housemaids and cooks. If someone was a bit better off, we'd look up to them and it was, 'Yes Sir,' 'Yes Ma'am', no Christian names.

Down Church Street there was a lot of little cottages and one little shop had three steps to it – kept by Mrs Timms. Nowadays 5/- would have bought her entire stock — two pots of jam and two boxes of sweets. Then there was Ma Cox's with all these boxes of sweets and her cats sitting there – always one cat, sometimes two. I used to love going there for two pennyworth of coconut chips – pink and white.

We had five or six bakers' shops in the town and down there in Church Street we had a dairy and Blanks newsagents. My father was a volunteer fireman for 42 years and Mr Blanks was a fireman and so was Charlie Roast, the blacksmith. We used to love to get round there as kids 'cos he had all the front open, and we'd watch him make the sparks fly till somebody came along with a big shire horse and he'd say, 'Now come on, you kids, you go off.' There wasn't much room there then for us with a big shire horse to be shod.

Tom Bygrave had a horse-brake and the football club used to hire it for away matches — at Preston or Whitwell. A couple of dozen used to go down – the team and some spectators. He was a good horseman – he stabled his horses in Pond Lane and did a bit of dealing at markets. He kept The Bull's Head. One of his boys got killed in the First World War – my sister used to do his sums for him and he used to repay her by bringing her locust beans to chew on. They fed the horses on locust beans – but they were good to chew on.

There used to be an old chap lived down Church Street, owned a tricycle and then there was old Wappy Gentle – he was a little old shepherd – lived in California then moved to a little cottage on the hill. Dusty Love used to live in Prospect Terrace – he was the dustman and he had a barrel organ and his wife was a little woman and she used to go with him and turn the handle – they'd often play it during the day. He had a shade over his eye and somebody said the wife had leaned out of the upstairs window with a cup of tea and it landed on Dusty and cut him over the eye.

Sometimes when we came out of school we'd see Jimmy Temple in the street ringing his bell and crying out. He was a bill poster as well as the Town Crier. He used to tell us what was happening, if there was a drama group coming, if there was a play on at the Town Hall, if the water was going to be turned off and what time,

Norton End, looking down Bygrave Lane (now Icknield Way) towards The Black Eagle.

or if there was a politician coming to speak – any public announcements. He'd come along ringing his bell and calling out 'Oyez, oyez,' and he always finished with 'God save the King.' He wore a top hat, but I can't remember any other uniform.

We came to live at No.1 Church Street which is now incorporated in with the George and Dragon. We had a lot of fun there as children. It was a five-bedroomed house, outside toilet, of course, and it was separate from the hotel. One of the present two lounges was our front room.

My father had what is now Chapmans butcher's shop. It was a furniture shop – loads of furniture all piled up. Dad was also undertaker so we used to pop through the churchyard and see all the weddings and funerals.

We used to come down here to Pond Lane but we were forbidden to go beyond Pond Lane – it was Norton Street from there and it was like a slum. We used to go as far as Monks for a 'tuppenny and a penn'orth' which was marvellous fish and chips then. This building (Mulberry Court) was built on the site of an old brewery and when it was being built they bulldozed up these big tanks.

In Church Street alone there were 13 shops, four places of worship: St Mary's, the Friends Meeting House, a chapel and the one that's been pulled down in Pond Lane – United Reform; and we had five pubs – The Stag, The Star, The Bull's Head, which they

The Toll Bar public house on the Royston Road c. 1910. The field where the cows from Waterloo Farm grazed is on the right.

Hitchin Street showing The White Hart public house and cobbled pavement.

reckon is the oldest pub in Baldock, The Eight Bells, The George and Dragon, then across the road to The Bushell and Strike in Jackson Street, round the corner to The Black Eagle. I think at one time there were 29 pubs in Baldock for a population of 2,000. Someone said that in the old days, there were 160 alehouses and every fourth house had a licence to sell ale.

For many years my grandma kept The White Hart and if she took 3/9d on one day that was really marvellous. She was a lovely old soul and everyone knew her. I'd go there every day after school. She'd sit by the fire and say, 'Stir that fire. Make the sparks fly. Go up to Taylor's and get me a quarter of currants.' 'Oh Gran,' I'd say, 'I can't go in and buy a quarter of currants.' 'Yes you can,' she'd say, 'I haven't got my weights and scales and I know just how many currants I want to put in my cake.' Another thing that used to amuse me about her, she had very voluminous black skirts – black sateen they were – and I can't remember what started the conversation about this skirt, but she said, 'It's been very, very good; it's been turned twice.' I said, 'Well, it's back where it started then, Gran.' 'Oh no, it isn't,' she said, 'Oh no.' To her dying day she said it had been turned twice but she wouldn't have it was back where it started! They used to do that in those days – everyone had hand-me-down clothes.

I always say my father was one of the first Samaritans. He came home one night propping this chap up and sat him in the kitchen and my mother said, 'Whatever are you doing, man?' So Dad says, 'He's drunk.' Mum says, 'I can see that, I can see he's drunk, but who is he?' So he says, 'Well I met him in The White Hart a few

times and he's a decent sort of chap, but he's been crossed in love.' So he says, 'I'll just put him to bed for the night and he'll be as sober as a judge in the morning.' So Dad put him to bed in one of the bedrooms that overlooked the churchyard and it had bars on the windows because when the Pattersons lived there it would have been a nursery. Mum said, 'Lock his door, for heaven's sake, I shan't sleep a wink – you don't know who he is.' So Dad locked him in and said, 'I'll take him a cup of tea in the morning, he'll be all right.' So he took him a cup of tea; he got up and used my father's razor. At lunchtime he went round The White Hart with Dad. He was quite smart – he was a groom to a titled lady in Stevenage and he had a straw boater. He came back to Sunday lunch – and he only stayed 16 years! He lived with us for *16 years* until he died – he was a good old sort. Very clean. He always sang 'The Sunshine of Your Smile,' or 'Little Grey Home in the West' every time he was shaving.

I can remember all the lovely trees we had in Baldock when I was a child. We had many, many more trees than we have now – the whole of Mansfield Road, (New Road then), was beautifully tree-lined, it was almost like an archway. In fact, sometimes I was a bit terrified of going down there — there was only Webb's Farm at the end but it was always pretty dark.

They must have taken a lot of trees down when the Mansfield Road houses were built. The same was true of Weston Way along from Webb's Farm to Willian Way. It was all trees because it was a ritual on Sunday night after Church, for us to go for a walk with Mum and Dad along the High Street and all the way round.

Tree-lined New Road, later to become Mansfield Road, with stone chippings piled along the side ready for re-surfacing.

My father purchased the bakery in Pinnocks Lane before the First World War. He became a steward of the Wesleyan Church, and later on, circuit steward of the Methodist Church. He was a governor of Pond Lane School where the headmaster was G N Bennett. His eldest son, Leslie, sold his first Model-T Ford Van in 1915 to my father.

My father used to graze our horses in front where the old mansion stood in the Park, which is now the site of Tesco's. When I was about 5 years old in 1916, the elm trees came down during a gale smashing our front windows and fence in Pinnocks Lane and I had glass in my hair. The meadow opposite, where the trees came down, was used for the horses which were let out from Heath Hall Farm.

Bread was quite short during the First World War and my father told me he had to put potato in it. At one time bread would be distributed to the poor by the Fifteen Houses Charity. A table would stand just inside the church porch, covered with a white cloth and the newly-baked loaves of bread would be put on it – they would smell lovely – Mr Hubbard, the verger, would distribute them. Hanscombes provided 6 or 12 large loaves and my father (Mr Juffs) provided 12 small loaves, but he never accepted the money for them. After a while the bread was distributed on the round. It finished in 1958.

Prospect Terrace, also known as 'The Ten Houses', in Clothall Road, prior to the First World War.

Also the old ladies who were recipients were supposed to receive so many yards of red flannel, but, of course, as time went by, nobody wanted red flannel, so at Christmastime they would receive a sum of money, in lieu, but gradually the value of that dwindled.

The great storm and blizzard of 1916 brings a tree down onto Prospect Terrace.

There were lots of little yards with houses tucked away behind the main streets — Pantile Yard, Colemans Court, Barkers Yard . . .

There was a private school in Bury House, then College House in Hitchin Street was another private school. Grove House School was in Whitehorse Street, and Oak House, also in Whitehorse Street, was a school.

I remember the horse-drawn fire engine and the horses would have to be run up the street to the fire station when the fire bell rang.

When I was very small there was a wash-house in Bygrave Lane and we had to sort out which days we could do the washing. There were just two coppers for us all to use. We were born to it so didn't think it was particularly hard.

There was a farm at the bottom of Royston Road and Billy Sale had a farm in the town and they used to cut the corn on one of his fields opposite us in Clothall Road. One of the lads in Prospect Terrace was down there picking up the corn one day and Billy Sale was on his horse and chased the boy all round the field. And the women from the Terrace went after him because the kid wasn't doing any harm really – yes, there was an uproar.

Alice Sale used to visit the houses and she had her own district and she called herself the District Visitor and she used to come round on Monday mornings. We went to Sunday School and church, but, of course, my mother never got time and she came round and said to my mother, 'How is it I never see you in Church, Bowskill?' Now that used to aggravate me to death. So my Mother said, 'I've no doubt, Miss Sale, I shall get to heaven as fast as you do, you don't have to go to church to be a Christian.'

Infants and Juniors 1902.

*Park Street Church of
England School c. 1900.*

*Most children in Baldock went to either the National School in Park
Street (known as the 'top school') or the British School in Pond Land
(the 'bottom school'). The school in Park Street was the Church of
England School and the Pond Lane school was more for the 'chapel-
goers' or 'nonconformists'. Geography also came into it, as it often
happened that children were sent to their nearest school, irrespective
of their parents' religious beliefs.*

Before 1914 I went to Pond Lane School – Bennett was the headmaster. There are only five that were at school with me who could
still be alive now.

There were very few games at school. I used to play football
years ago. In Hitchin Street, there was a private school where Mrs
de Bathe lived and one of the boys told me that they did play
those boys at football, but that had petered out before I got there.
I've got a faint recollection that a man called Hartley or Harley ran
it – it was called something college (College School). Children of
shopowners went there and they were stuck up.

We didn't mix much with the boys from the other school. There
was quite a lot of bitterness between us. They thought we was on
a lower grade – they were the top school up at Park Street. We
never had no books. We just had a slate and as our teacher got
older, the noise of the slates squeaking used to get on his nerves
and he'd say, 'Sharpen those pencils.' But some boys could do it
deliberately and we'd have to rub our pencils on a V-shaped block
of wood that had some metal on it and you rubbed the pencil up
and down and put a point on it so it didn't squeak so much.

When I first started school in Pond Lane, my teacher was Miss
Blaxall – she became Mrs Grimston. She courted a young chap in
khaki and he used to come into the classroom and have a chat
with us – that's before they were married.

I've been up Pond Lane once or twice now and had a look at the
old school and I remember my days there, sharpening the pencils,
slate pencils for the infants and there were some old buildings
nearby with the blacksmith's block still there and the open fire.
Mr Bennett the headmaster used to keep his bike there. We'd get
told to do things – two sharpening pencils, two for cleaning the
playground, two for cleaning lavatories – we didn't mind 'cos we
escaped prayers at 9 o'clock and we used to go down there and
sharpen the pencils and we'd get the box out and look through it
and say, 'that one wants doing, that's all right and that's all right
and there's another one there'; I don't suppose we did more than
half-an-hour and the rest of the time we spent riding on his bike
round the block 'til a quarter-to-ten and he never knew – I don't
remember being caught. But he was a nice old chap, Mr Bennett.

School went up to Standard 6 and when I was in Standard 4 we
had a teacher, old Mr Young, and he didn't buy any canes. He

Park Street schoolboys being taught the tasks that the man did round the house, from mending shoes and cleaning out the gutters to sieving coal-dust and chopping sticks for firewood.

used to send one of us up the highway to cut one out of the hedge – one with a few knots in it. He used to chew tobacco whilst he taught us and I was sitting in the front desk and all of a sudden I got such a wallop for doing something or other, and I put me head on the desk and I felt someone sidle up to me and it were Mr Young and he gave me a peppermint. He was a hard man but soft with it. Same as Mr Bennet, he gave me a wallop once when he found me with me Sexton Blake inside my copy book and I rushed out the door and went home. I don't remember what happened after that. One bloke though didn't do nothing else but read Sexton Blake and Buffalo Bills – they couldn't do anything with him. He was left to his own devices after a time. He joined the army after he left school – he lived up Clarkes Yard in the cottages there. I think he died while he was in the army – he was only in his early 20s and they brought him home and his family asked if I'd like to see him, so I did.

I went to the Church of England Park Street School. Miss Christopher was my headmistress – she'd give me a cough sweet if I had a cold.

During the war we had a lot of Belgian children here and we'd play skipping – 'salt, mustard, vinegar, pepper', 'un, deux, trois', 'Here we come gathering nuts in May'. Of course there was always hopscotch and playing with a top and we had a hoop and a scooter. But we weren't allowed to wander very far – it was straight home from school on account of the war.

At school I used to have a teacher called Jessie and one called Phyllis and I used to think the sun shone out of those two, I really did. We only learnt the three R's and a bit of sewing and a bit of drawing and we had a fair amount of religion which I always enjoyed because they used to have an easel with all those lovely shiny pictures on – American cloth they used to call it. She would turn them over one at a time – the Good Samaritan, the Flight into Egypt, the Nativity and I've never forgotten those pictures. I can visualise them today.

They talk about what they must have in schools today, the huge playing fields – we had a gravel or shingle playing patch about the area of this flat. We all had to play in that and you fell over and cut your knees nearly every day – we didn't have anything like what they have today. I read in the paper the other day, they put some children through a simple test – arithmetic or reading and they couldn't do it. I could have done it standing on my head. We had it drummed into us – times tables, reading and you said it over and over again and you never forgot it. We'd take jacket potatoes because there was a huge old-fashioned fire and we'd put the potatoes under there and have them at lunchtime. If we didn't do that, we'd take a ha'penny or a penny down to Hanscombes and

Park Street pre-World War I with a schoolboy (left) standing at the entrance to Pepper Alley.

get a currant bun. I can see Netty Hanscombe now. She'd come out with a big tray of buns and she'd get a huge tin of treacle or golden syrup and a distemper brush and she'd dip this distemper brush in and go all over the buns and then put sugar on the top. But if she had a lady come in, say one of the class of Baldock I suppose you'd call them, she'd say, 'Now come on you kids, stand up against that wall,' and we had to stand by that wall 'til she'd served this lady. And there we were, by this wall, with the bell going to ring at any minute and we'd have to tear back up Pepper Alley to get back to school.

There weren't the discipline problems then because the discipline was always carried out at home before you got to school. We weren't allowed to speak at the meal table and certainly not with your mouth full, nor read at table. My sister who loved reading, I remember once brought a book to the table and she kept having a sly look at it thinking my father wouldn't notice. But he did – told her to stop reading – but she carried on. He told her three times and finally leaned over, picked up the book and threw it on the fire – and it was a library book!

Pony and trap in the High Street c. 1910. Note the white lion on the roof of the pub.

Outside of school hours, children had to make their own amusements. Mother didn't want them round her skirts whilst she tackled the numerous household chores, and father wanted a 'bit of peace and quiet' when he came home from work. So groups of friends would get together to devise ways of passing the time — skipping (boys and girls), whipping tops, kicking a tennis ball, or digging up dandelion roots to earn a penny or two.

The town was so different in those days. We used to play football in the High Street. I used to get up there – I was a bit young but these boys would put their coats down and play a game of football with a tennis ball. If you saw a car, everyone would turn and look at it. Then in the winter there'd be one big slide right down the middle of the High Street with all the little old boys sliding on it. That's going back 70 odd years. If a pony and trap came by, you just got out of the way of it.

After the harvest we used to go into the fields and dig up the dandelion roots and clean them and take them to the herbalist in the

A school party enjoying a picnic in Avenue Field.

town, and he used to buy them off us. I think they went to Ransoms in Hitchin. We collected camomile too and hips. Later on we'd get blackthorn and elderberries and crab apples to make jam and wine. We'd always go and pinch the walnuts by throwing sticks up the trees, but the walnuts used to stain our hands and when a complaint was made to the school our teacher knew who it was by the state of our hands, so we used to get the cane. If we knew it was coming we would hide the cane in the piano. And you didn't dare tell your mum 'cos you'd get another one. The policemen used to keep a watch out, too, and they might tell you off a bit – there was PC Flower – we used to call him Hollyhock – he'd be on the Cross sometimes, directing traffic, and Sergeant Gray lived in Hitchin Street – that's where the Police Station was then.

In the summer we had seven weeks' holiday from school to work in the fields. We only got about eighteen pence a week, I think. One year when the weather had been bad, they were carrying corn down the High Street on top of carts on October 2 – Baldock Fair Day – it was a very late harvest that year. Another year there was snow at Baldock Fair.

My earliest memories are of playing in the churchyard as kids and being chased by poor old Johnny Cawdell for playing on the gravestones, the flat ones. We lived in that private part of The George and Dragon which wasn't part of the hotel then. It was a big house really and that front room that they use as a bar was then our main living room.

We'd come out of the house with our tops and whips or our hoops and we'd roll them right up the High Street without meeting a soul until perhaps we met our grandfather coming from the brewery, leading his old horse and cart on his way to The White Hart for his dinner. Jolly old soul he was – used to swear a bit – but he was very kind-hearted.

Father kept the shop on the other side of the road, he sold second-hand furniture and he was also the undertaker. He also used to put the Christmas tree up for the Sunday School children, and Mr Nairn who was the curate then, often said, 'Albert, we see your wife and children in church but we never see you!' 'I come at Christmas,' he says, 'and I always put the Christmas tree up, so I do my share.'

We were very friendly with Eva Carter, Ivy Gray, the policeman's daughter and others and we had skipping contests down the High Street – about six of us – and if one of us owned a penny we went to Ma Cox's sweet shop and bought a sherbert dab as a prize and whoever won the race got the sherbert dab, but only on condition we all had a lick.

My sister, Kit, was a wizard with a top and, of course, you could do it in the High Street in those days, and my dad would turn us out carrot tops and turnip tops on his lathe and she could whip these tops yards. She was an expert. You might see a hay cart come along or Reggie James or his brother Arthur, with his milk cart, or Juffs baker's cart but apart from that you didn't see any vehicles at all. And you just got out of the way for a minute if anything came along.

We didn't have a lot of books but I remember in the very early days when the Children's Newspaper came out, we had that, but we never got it to read until Dad had been all the way through it. He used to have a magazine called Titbits and we had the Sunday People. Dad had quite a few Dickens' books but they were beyond our reading then. We had various dolls, most of them home-made probably, and golliwogs, which are considered very controversial now — but we loved those. Mum used to make them out of black stockings and give them button eyes. But we didn't have any real dolls 'til we were about 13 or 14. I don't think we could afford them. We had a doll's pram which really belonged to my sister who was a bit of a tomboy and she never really liked pushing it 'til one day her friend was asked by her father to go and get some grit for the chickens. So they took this doll's pram to collect it and came back with half-a-hundred weight in the pram, the springs all broken.

We had games like Ludo and a pack of cards to play 'Beat your Neighbour' and 'Snap' and we'd have five or six kids sitting round our big mahogany table cutting up cardboard. We'd go to Booths for cardboard boxes to make dolls' houses.

I came to Baldock in 1912 when I was three and we lived at the bottom of Church Street, then two years later moved to Prospect Terrace in Clothall Road with my sister and my parents.

We were always well-behaved and did what Mother told us. At five o'clock every evening she'd say, 'Your father's coming in for his tea now, be quiet.' And we were.

We used to bowl hoops and play hopscotch in Clothall Road, then we'd sit on the bank by the side of the road and play jacks.

One day I was in church and when the hymn was announced someone coughed and I didn't hear it, so I turned to my friend and asked her what the number was. Immediately I felt a bony finger right between my shoulder blades, it was Alice Sale and she hissed, 'Stop talking, girl.' Well when I got to school the next day, I found that she'd been round there and told Miss Taylor, so I was called out in front of the class and got my face slapped both sides.

My grandmother lived in one of the old houses at the back of the town – the first house opposite the Orange Tree. We had a tuck shop like I used to read about in Frank Richards' books. Ernie Ellis – who was interested in the drama group in Baldock – his mother used to keep it and sold toffee-apples and the like and I remember going down on a Christmas morning to get something like that. It was where the little churchyard is near what used to be

Bygrave's stables in Pond Lane (now no. 18). There used to be some tombstones there 'cos those stables used to be a chapel and we respected it, but the only time I went over was if our ball went over from the playground. Those stables of Bygrave's looked in good order – he used to keep the Bull's Head.

They lived in a yard at the bottom of Church Street – old Toby Scales lived there and we used to get a ha'porth of sweets smelling of paraffin 'cos he used to serve paraffin out of the same room.

I can't tell you much about the games children played in the street because we weren't allowed out – that was my mother, she wouldn't let us go out and play or mix with Baldock people – we had to play in the garden – just with balls and skipping ropes. I had two brothers and two sisters. My brothers had no more freedom than we did, not until they left school and started work. We didn't go scrumping or anything like that. I think we should have been burning in hell if we had!

Washing, cooking and cleaning were all part of the weekly routine and took up the larger part of a woman's day. She still had to find time for other things, too, like brewing home-made wine and making rugs and clothes from anything that came to hand. The children were expected to help as well to stretch the family's income as far as possible.

Monday morning we used to fill the copper before we went to school and that was quite a step from the pump outside the back door to the shed where Mum did the washing. Then we'd come home for dinner and have to hang the washing out while Mum got ready to do another load. And we'd have to wash up before going back to school – you washed up in a bowl on the table, not in a sink – the water was outside and we'd heat it over the fire. Then we'd have to do the mangling – three times the towels would have to go through and so many times for pillowslips and sheets. They were all white as the driven snow – and it was only soda and soap and elbow-grease and Reckitt's Blue. We always used to have to get the thumb blue because Mum said the squares made it gritty. It was a bit dearer than the squares which were in their own little bag. With the thumb blue you had to make your own bag. And we used soap – Sunlight and Preservine. You used to grate it or shave it with a knife and Mother used Four E's – 'Four E's for Ease', the slogan was.

If Mum was doing collars she'd put starch in. Then the iron would be heated on the fire. There was always a bit of hessian on the floor to rub the iron on to cleanse it before she started ironing. Mum worked from morn 'til night but she still had time to teach us to knit and sew, and read to us; and when we could read, she'd pick out a book so that when she was ironing we'd sit and read to her.

'When SUNLIGHT SOAP is
in the tub,
You needn't boil, nor toil,
nor scrub.'

The staff of Baldock Post Office, 1911.

Then in the winter evenings we'd make the old peg rugs. Dad was on the post and summer and winter they'd change the uniform, a thicker one for winter and a thinner one for summer and the old one would be discarded. Well Mum used to keep the jackets because they had red piping on them and we'd have to sit and unpick the piping so she could make patterns in the rugs. And then if my brother was home, he'd get out his violin or tin whistle and we'd have a sing-song around the fire. My other brother had a paper round and saved enough money to buy a mouth organ, so we were in our element. And they had to do errand boy jobs as well – walked with baskets – they didn't have a bike – you were well in if you had a bike.

We'd go and get half-a-leg of mutton or lamb on a Saturday and if that came to 1/1d we had to take it back – it couldn't be more than a shilling. That would last us 'til about Tuesday because Mum would make a stew or soup with the bones. With vegetables and three pennyworth of pieces and a pennyworth of suet you'd have a good stew and you didn't want anything else.

We never had tripe – threepennyworth of liver sometimes. Fish came round on a cart. We had bloaters – and the oil that came out of them! And something that strikes me now – you could always smell what people had for dinner or breakfast – you could smell the bacon cooking – now you can't smell anything. And I'm sure it doesn't taste as good.

My mother had to light the fire every day to cook by. She had a spit and hung the meat on it with a dish in front to catch the grease. And we had another dish we put herrings on. She made suet puddings and sometimes we'd come home from school and say, 'What've you got to eat, Mum, we're hungry?' And she'd say, 'There's a couple of swimmers in the pot,' — they were little bits of suet crust; we'd put sugar on them and eat them and still eat our dinner.

She worked hard – there were five bedrooms to look after and three girls and my father, and during the war she had a lady to come in and help her make the beds – we had soldiers billeted on us and she tried to give them all a bed – just mattresses on the floor, of course. Washing was done in the copper in the scullery. She had to light the fire underneath it and washing lasted all day. She would take it round to The White Hart, which was kept by my grandmother, to dry it. Of course, everything was white in those days, white sheets and white nightdresses and white underclothes. There was a lot of starching and blueing.

My mother's father worked for the brewery – he was a maltster. He sometimes worked in the brewery and sometimes at the maltings in Whitehorse Street. They used to cook snails on the wall of this big kiln.

My grandmother lived in one of the cottages near the church-yard which were pulled down when the new Pond Lane houses were built. She used to come through there to go to The White Hart to get a jug of beer and we used to say to her, 'Aren't you afraid, Granny, to come through the churchyard at this time of night, all on your own?' And she'd say, 'Well, the living might hurt you, but the dead can't.'

Kitchen interior pre-1914 showing the range used for cooking and heating.

Bygrave Lane c. 1914.

Father had a shoe shop at the corner of Sun Street and we lived over the shop. I've heard Mum say they were foreigners in Baldock and that's why he didn't make a go of it so he got into the Post Office as an auxiliary postman and we still lived there. Then we moved from there, when Dad sold the business, to Royston Road, to the maltings cottage.

I used to wear lots of petticoats and boots and stockings, summer and winter and we'd be out in the fields gleaning during the summer holidays, all round Norton Road and round to the hills. On Sunday evenings after Dad came out of chapel they would take us for walks all round so that we could see where the fields had been cleared so we could go gleaning the next day.

It was a very strict upbringing – prayers and bible readings. I wouldn't wish it on anybody – it didn't make any impression on us, we didn't get any enjoyment out of it. We had to sing grace at table; but were we pleased with what we got? I often think about that – were we – should we have been thankful for what we had?

Mum used to make wine but we never had any and she'd take a drop occasionally, but father wouldn't. She made all sorts, elder, hips, cowslip and any of the fruits we could get. I think she used to do it in case anybody ever came in. It was all in a day's work. Everything revolved round the home – apart from going to church and work. All their time was spent at home. And you see all those five weeks of school holiday that we spent gleaning, Mum used to thrash all that corn out and give it to Mrs Saville who lived in the house next to the Vic – there was a farm there and she used to buy it from us and maybe that money would buy one of us a pair of boots.

Our parents used to eat young stinging nettles, about the top inch-and-a-half – they're very good for the blood. Elderberries and elderflower were also collected and still are. Elderflower makes a lovely wine, like a light German wine.

Mother used soda for cleaning and Sunlight soap. She did her washing in a copper. We had running water in the kitchen but only cold water. We had a bathroom put in while we were there. We had a big brown sink when we first moved in. Food was plainer but nicer, more flavour. Often everything was cooked all in one dixie. We had a range at the Black Eagle where we cooked. You had to work out how hot the fire would be so that the temperature would be just right for the cake. I remember my mother putting a piece of paper in the oven – she could tell how hot the oven was by how quickly the paper turned brown.

People were often content but on Monday, Tuesday, Wednesday and Thursday there wasn't much to eat, just bread and scrape. People would buy 2oz of bacon and ask for it to be put on the slate.

The sweep lived just a couple of doors away from us – Tommy Barcock, and our chimney had to be swept every seven or eight weeks, it was so blocked up. My mum used to say to Dad, 'Here, don't shovel any more coal on that fire, you're not at the brewery now.' And when my dad went to work at six o'clock, my mum would say to him, 'Give old Barcock a knock or else he won't come.' So Dad knocked him up and he came round and swept our chimney. We always had plenty of beer at our house – no one drank much of it, but old Barcock could drink his share. He used to drink it as he swept the chimney and the more he drank, the more he talked – it would take him a long time to sweep that chimney. He was a good horseman – he was a good sweep and he'd only got one arm.

We only had a scrubbing brush and pail to get things clean and Lifebouy soap and the white hearthstone. There used to be a man lived down the bottom end of the town – Whirly Jellis. He had a donkey and he'd go out with the donkey and cart. Jellis used to lay up Bygrave Street, (now Icknield Way) making hearth balls from the chalk and he'd sell them to the shops and he got a living doing that, but he never did a day's regular work. We used to see him on the side of the road when we went to Litlington to visit an uncle. The donkey grazed by the hedge while old Jellis made hearth balls – he may have heated them, but they were lovely and white when they got to the shops. On Saturday I worked for Browns. We had to sweep paths up and Bertha Brown, the lady who owned it gave me three or four bowls of gruel to take to the poor people in Norton Street.

Christmas was a time for families to get together and most people were able to afford something a bit special to add to the normal daily fare. But presents were few and far between.

We didn't have any treats at Christmas and I never had a toy but as far as I'm concerned, we couldn't have had a better home, as poor as we were. Father worked for the Brewery and at Christmas we had an apple and an orange and perhaps a bag of nuts. Mother was a wonderful cook and worked in a farmhouse as a girl. My aunt said to me, 'You know your mother was wise, whenever she changed her job, she always went to a farmhouse, for the simple reason that you got good food at a farmhouse.' She said that if you went to work for a vicar at the vicarage, they were as poor as church mice and you was half-starved.

The farmers always provided for themselves in those days. They'd kill a cow or a bullock or whatever it was – they made 'ay in those days. But someone had to prepare the food for them, so they came in for the luxuries, too – whatever was left over. They didn't eat together, they had theirs in the kitchen. My mother really kept us going, what she made out of chicken you couldn't make out of a turkey today. Really lovely it was.

At Christmas time we were not allowed to know what presents we were going to have, we never had many parcels. Weeks before we'd hide a bit of candle end because we always had to take a candle up to bed at night, and at about one or two on Christmas morning my sister would say, 'He's been'. And we'd burn the string off with the candle – it's a wonder we didn't set everything alight.

Christmastime at Worbey's the butcher's in Church Street.

*United Reformed Church,
Whitehorse Street, built 1904.*

*South Road, formerly Clarkes
Lane, with Caleb Lunn and
his oil barrow.*

We had family do's at Christmas – Mum had six brothers and two sisters and I think three of the brothers lived at Stotfold. They brought Brussels sprouts and celery – whatever was available. Then they'd say, 'Is there anything left in the whisky bottle.' We had a lot of fun – lots of relations calling in and Granny had a sister at Wood Green and she always came for Christmas. She was great fun, we'd never met anyone like her – colourful language – and Aunt Min used to egg her on.

We didn't make much of Christmas – except Mother would send us up to Izzards in Pembroke Road – she used to make mincemeat there – and we'd take a jam-jar and get two penn'orth of mincemeat in it. Izzards were bakers. Harry Izzard used to go round with oil and all sorts and he had an old man, name of Caleb Lunn, working for him who used to go round with the oil.

We didn't have any treats or toys. We would have an orange in our stocking at Christmas with a few ashes to fill it out, but oranges were a luxury in those days, so were bananas and tomatoes.

I had a Hornby Train Set as a boy. Later on, when I was working, we'd make lots of Christmas cakes, people bought them more than they do now, I think, and we'd also bake Christmas dinner for people who couldn't get theirs in their ovens. This lasted well into the 30s and I often couldn't get away 'til after three in the afternoon to have my own Christmas dinner and be with the children.

I remember the gypsies coming round and singing 'God Rest Ye Merry Gentlemen' and they'd come round the bakery sometimes asking for stale bread.

The majority of people in Baldock were employed either on the farms, in the shops, in the big houses or in the brewing and malting trade. Elmwood Manor was the largest of the big houses and stood in its own grounds, with an adjacent deer park. It had a large staff of servants and was a small community in itself.

I remember Elmwood Manor, it stood derelict. Before the First World War when the soldiers were on manoeuvres, they took over in the Park. They used it for accommodation. The previous owner, as I've heard it, was named Beldam – he lived there. It belonged to the Pryors of Weston and that was the start of the Park being opened up. It was all private before that. When the Bondor came and took over the building, that was a different environment altogether.

Mother was born at Cottered and she was in service at Elmwood Manor from the age of 13½. She was quite overwhelmed with what a lovely place it was. They had a coachman, footman, housemaids, parlour-maids and she went as under-kitchen maid. Anyway she got on quite well with cook apparently – they had a terrible housekeeper – everyone was petrified of her and the head butler – they were a couple – everyone was frightened to death of them.

The housekeeper said to my mum one day, 'Kate, I want you to feed this old lady.' She was one of the household, infirm and couldn't feed herself, so the housekeeper said, 'It's a job to get her to eat so you must insist on it and feed her.' Mum was only about 14 then and she went upstairs in great trepidation because this old woman was an autocratic old devil. She sat in bed and she wouldn't eat this – it was chopped up chicken – and Mum got so frightened because the housekeeper had said she *must* eat it. So Mum ate it all and when she went down, the housekeeper said what a good girl she was for getting the old lady to eat all the food. She was frightened to death that she'd get the sack if they ever found out. So any time she was asked to go up and feed the old lady, if she wouldn't eat, Mum used to eat it up – pudding and all.

When visitors drew up in their carriages, the maids used to look down and watch them arrive. They had big balls there and she said it was just like a little community on its own – like a little village – with all those servants. They used to have lovely times there with all the parties and balls and everything. A lot of hanky panky went on there, I reckon, with footmen and the maids and all this, that and t'other.

But she used to have to take water upstairs every morning because there were these two girls there – they were sisters – Beldams. They were very plain girls with ever such spotty faces and they used to put oatmeal all over their faces. My mother said they frightened her to death when she went in their bedrooms and they had this oatmeal all over their faces. They were big girls with big feet and she was frightened to death of them.

Overleaf: Elmwood Manor, 1912, which was destroyed by fire 1916.
Top Left: Arthur Buck, Head Gardener at Elmwood Manor with pony pulling the lawn mower.
Centre: Entrance Hall to Elmwood Manor.
Right: The Drawing Room.

They had lovely dinner parties and they were more or less self-supporting, because they had their own laundry and I think they must have had a farm and a big dairy. In fact the dairy was the only part left after the fire. But Mum said they always had loads of fresh cream and eggs. They had to make the butter once a week and she had to churn it. They had vast gardens because Mum said they used to have lovely asparagus, and grapes out of the vinery. When the table was laid for a dinner party, they all used to sneak down and have a look at all the silver and the gold laid out. My Mum loved it there – she had a lovely life – well, of course, it was for her because she came out of a little farm worker's cottage. It must have been like going in paradise.

There were three of them in the kitchen at Elmwood and they had three little iron beds right at the top of the house. It was ever so poky and it was very sparse – lino on the floor and rough old blankets and sheets, but it was clean and they didn't expect anything more in those days.

The servants were very well fed and Mum said that about once or twice a week some of the very poor people used to come to the back door with a pillow case and they used to put bread in it for them and give them a can of soup because they always had soup cooking there. They had two or three cooks. They were very good to the Baldock people. Mum loved it there – the only problem was this terrible housekeeper and the butler. The housekeeper used to see the lady of the house every day and then go down to the kitchen to issue orders for the day's menus, but she always had to knock at the kitchen door. There was a very strict hierarchy. And no one could go into the butler's pantry without permission. Mother was only allowed to do certain things like prepare the vegetables and clean all the pans and the kitchen, until she got a little higher up and she was allowed to do other things. They all had to take hot water in big brass cans up to the bedrooms, two or three flights of stairs. She also had to go round with the housemaid – the one who made the beds and they had to empty the slops, wipe the chamber pots out and put them back in the little cupboards and clean all the wash-basins.

She had to get up about 5 o'clock to clear all the clinkers out and light the fires and then prepare the big breakfasts that they had every day. She said on the sideboard they had porridge and grape nuts, kedgeree, bacon, eggs, kidneys, kippers, toast, so many things. Every day!

We got caught in the old park once – Elm Park. The gardener, Buck his name was, used to live in the lodge – he caught us several times. A policeman caught us once and I had a sackful of wood – just little pieces. I ran and he pretended to take our names, but he didn't do anything. I tipped the wood out so's if he caught us I wouldn't have anything on me to show I'd been there.

I remember Elmwood Manor when I was a girl – the band used to play in there on a Sunday afternoon. Baldock had a silver town band then. The Hergerts were a big noise in that. The two lads and the father were there and a man named Crouch, lived in Pembroke Road, he was an undertaker and he used to play the silver cornet. The public were admitted to the park on a Sunday afternoon – there was deer and all sorts there. You went in by the gate at the little lodge on the High Street.

It was Epiphany when it burnt down. We were in church singing an Epiphany hymn when the fire bell went and we were dying to get out of church to see what was burning.

I can remember Elmwood Manor being all a-blaze. As a matter of fact at one time we had a photograph of it with the flames pouring out of all the windows; you see my father was a fireman for 42 years. My mother always said that it was to have been a finishing school for young ladies, but two or three nights before they were due to come, and all the ground fittings were in, something started the fire off and it all went up in flames. It stood derelict for years until the photographic people took it on and then the Bondor came.

At one time there were three breweries in the town and several maltings, and working in the industry was an attractive proposition as there was usually plenty of free beer to be had.

Father stayed at the brewery in World War One, he was a stoker. He stoked the fires that boiled the water and pumped it up into the big vat above where they did the brewing; it was an important job, you had to keep a constant temperature. Two days he had to go in at 3 o'clock – he never had an alarm clock (Tuesday and Thursday I think). We only lived in a two-room cottage and I slept in the same room as my father for a long time and I never knew him to have an alarm. He'd turn over in his grave if he knew the

Baldock Fire Brigade standing in front of the burnt-out shell of Elmwood Manor.

Workers at Simpson's Brewery holding the tools of their trade.

brewery had gone. The only time they went to the sea was when Simpsons had an outing. Mother never went when we were tiny but when we were older she used to go.

My father's family came from Wellbury and he used to walk from there to Stead's Brewery in Pond Lane every day and home again over the fields. He would carry a lantern in the dark. After the fire at Stead's, father transferred to Simpsons.

The Brewery was probably the biggest employer for many years. Uncle Alf worked there as a night watchman and he'd have to go round and watch the vats in case they all frothed up and he'd have to stop it going over the floor.

I never went inside the brewery but I can remember watching the sacks of malt go up on the hoist. I think every child in Baldock used to stand and watch those and the Foden steam lorries that used to go in and out. They used horse-drawn drays, too, for a while alongside the steam lorries. It must have employed a fair number of people – it wasn't just the brewing, there were the coopers making the barrels as well, and people washing the bottles.

My grandfather worked in the maltings, he was a malt maker and I used to go into work with him sometimes on a Sunday. He had to go in because the fuel had to be made up and the malt lying on the floor still had to be turned. He worked where Taylors' Fish and Chip shop is. They had a big wooden rake and shovel for turning the malt. I don't know how many men they employed, there was only my grandfather there on a Sunday. I wonder whether it was a healthy way to live. There were low ceilings and the atmosphere was always moist with the barley drying out. I remember looking through the shutters occasionally and watching them turn the malt. He had to wear canvas boots with rope soles. I can't remember when it stopped working, it was still there in the early twenties.

There were more than twenty pubs at one time. I could count 27. The Victoria Pub used to be called The Sun. Simpsons had several maltings – two in the High Street and one on the corner of Whitehorse Street and Clothall Road. The barley would go in and it had to be turned in the heat by three or four people. You could often get a warm near the maltings. Pages had maltings up the Royston Road, they lived in Hitchin Street.

The barley used to be carted up to the brewery and pulled up to the top by a chain ready for dropping in when they made the beer.

There was nothing to do except work for the brewery or on the farms. Letchworth was a godsend to us for work. At the weekends we would look around Letchworth to see it developing. In the week there was a continual flow of people coming down the cinder path from Letchworth to the Baldock pubs as Letchworth hadn't got any. It helped the publicans in Baldock.

Mr and Mrs Derman at The Barley Mow in Clothall – she used to keep a monkey. Lots of people made home-made wine and it was sold in the bar, too.

Getting around was quite difficult unless you could afford to travel by train. Most people walked or hitched a ride, so they looked largely to the town for their entertainment.

Most of the time if you wanted to get around anywhere, you had to walk. That's what I had to do until I got a bike at 19. There were no buses previous to the First World War. Simpsons delivered beer to Luton and my father got me a lift to Luton when I went there for a week's holiday. Four horses dragged a big brake to Luton a few times a week. When they got to the bottom of Offley Hill, they stopped and the driver had to whistle to get them to make water before climbing the hill. The train service was good. If you had the money you could travel by train.

Staff and passengers at Baldock Railway Station.

The first motor car I ever saw belonged to a gentleman that was married to one of my father's sisters. They had a farm at Bell Bar near Potters Bar and they came to Baldock to show the new car off. He parked it outside our dining room window (at the top of Church Street) and there was dozens of kids from nowhere to see this motor car – they'd never seen one. He was Uncle Jack and he'd shoo them all away and five minutes later they'd all be back. Then I remember there was another gentleman in Baldock – his name was Johnny Winepress and he had the next motor car that I saw and he was courting a Baldock woman, name of Bonfield.

About 1904 the bicycle became popular, and Fred Butler had these bicycles and they were expensive, £3 or £4. You could pay in instalments. Before then they'd had to walk to work – to Sandon or wherever. But they had to learn to ride these bikes first and every dinnertime the bikes used to come out for a bit of a practice. Most of them got on all right with them, riding up and down the High Street, but old Harry Crawshaw couldn't come to terms with it – he was a bit sharp-tongued. Down the High Street he came – couldn't get around the corner to get into Whitehorse Street and Pattersons had got all these harnesses outside and old Harry couldn't stop so he came off and went over the top into these harnesses. And that finished him as a cyclist, he wouldn't ride the bike no more and the bike had to go back.

Baldock Cross c. 1910. Pattersons catered for all kinds of transport from horses to cycles and motor cars.

If you wanted to go out of the town before the First World War, it was either train or Shanks's pony. We'd sometimes go to Hitchin Market by train with Mother – 3d that was – but it was a real good outing. We'd stand by the crockery man and watch him, shouting out. Mum got her false teeth in Hitchin Market.

The Rose and Crown would meet the trains with their horse and carts and most of the big houses kept their own horses and carts – like the Morrises at the Wilderness. People had to walk everywhere. My uncle would walk from Wellbury across to Wallington, down to Ashwell Station and then on to Litlington. Bob Ridley's father was a carrier – he went to Hitchin each day and fetched and carried for people.

The one blessing for us was Baker's Close. You could go up there after you'd finished work in an old pair of boots and if someone could provide a football you were all right. In the summer someone ran a cricket team. Previous to the First World War, Baldock had a very good cricket team and the cricket pitch was where the school is in Weston Way. It belonged to Mr Morris and he lived in the Wilderness and he used to have ladies come down from London – he must have been influential – and he'd bring a team down from London. They would play the locals and Baldock would play Royston and Hitchin and the likes of them. It was a private cricket pitch. You could go in and watch but if you saw an apple fall off the tree you couldn't go and pick it up, or else out the gate you went.

I used to play for the Social Club – the boys' team – all good comrades and if the town team was short, we were sometimes asked to make up the team, but we had to go under another name because

Baldock Juniors Football Team 1911-12.

BALDOCK JUNIORS

it wasn't legal, see. We were in a league. The first year, the league was split up into two divisions and we played Kimpton or Whitwell and we won – on Hitchin Town ground.

The Social Club went on in the evening – it was a blessing for Baldock boys. They had a billiard table and that kept boys off the streets and out of the pubs. Mr Newling did a wonderful job for us, he devoted himself to the old boys. No gambling or anything like that. I think he kept more boys on the straight where they might have gone into the pubs – we've got a lot to be grateful to him for.

I've got a photograph of an aeroplane, it came down at Baldock over night and we got up early in the morning and saw it off. I always thought that it was this plane – with the pilot, Captain Hamilton – that crashed at Graveley but some say there's some doubt, so I wouldn't argue with that.

In the early days there was an annual sports fete. If they could get permission, they used the field at the bottom of Hitchin Street (Avenue Park). There were races – long races and short races. They had flower and produce shows but there was no Allotment Association then. Most of the competition was provided by the big houses. My wife's father was a professional gardener – he worked for Bishells – and the food would be sold at the end of the show. We lived in the last house in Orchard Road on the left-hand side. A travelling theatre came down and performed in a tent and they used to give some good old shows. 'Maria Marten and the Red Barn' and all those sorts of things. Then Charlie Barham came from Hitchin to start the cinema in Whitehorse Street. Barham's Bughut, we called it.

We'd go to the cinema in Whitehorse Street for 2d on a Saturday afternoon. I remember going to the silent films, with the piano playing, but it was wonderful when the talkies came in.

The aeroplane forced to land in Baldock during army manoeuvres 1912.

'The Baroness Whist Drive' in the Town Hall.

Lil Musk from The Chequers used to play at the old Baldock Cinema in Whitehorse Street and when you went courting you went in the love seats (double seats) in the back row of the cinema.

I remember the River Ivel – it ran from Baldock to Radwell – it overflowed one year and made a big lake in the field which also froze over, so one evening we didn't go to Bible Class, we went sliding on this lake and people came with proper skates from all around at night to skate there and they had hurricane lamps all round the sides so they could see in the moonlight.

There wasn't a lot of entertainment. There'd be whist drives and dances at the Town Hall and theatrical parties used to come in and stop for two or three days at the Town Hall.

We used to go to dances at Baldock Town Hall – sometimes five nights out of six – and if you paid 2/6 for a dance that was a really big do. The dances started during the First World War and we were only young but we were very tall and Aunt Min used to take us to these dances because we had a lot of very young South African soldiers here and they hadn't got enough females to go round. That's where I learnt to dance – these young South African soldiers taught me and Aunt Min taught us anything they left out.

Every Sunday night we used to go with Mum and Dad to Norton Fisheries – it was like a ritual. It was beautiful there – walking across the fields. Everyone went for a walk on Sunday evenings.

Norton Fisheries — a favourite Sunday evening walk.

I remember as a very little girl getting a bottle of lemonade and some sandwiches and going with a friend over the fields blackberrying. We'd be gone all day – just two little girls. We'd go to Norton Fisheries, too, with our lemonade and sandwiches just on our own, without our parents and go and paddle there.

October 2nd or 3rd was the one day of our lives – we used to run up the street to see who was coming and who wasn't and if you had 6d in your pocket, you were lucky. I didn't go on the roundabouts 'cos I spent mine on rock and nougat so I never got a ride. The fair was brought in by horse and cart before they got lorries. Vans were parked in town and the horses were put in fields to graze, then they went from Baldock to Nottingham for the Goose Fair.

Rides cost 1d or 2d and people would make a day of it from the villages. Sometimes they used to sell horses and ponies in Whitehorse Street on fair days in the early days. They would run them up and down the street to show them off.

We used to enjoy the fair – we watched them making the brown and white spit rock. Old Mrs Harris would swing it and roll it and put it on a hook then spit on her hands and pull it out again.

There weren't so many gaming machines but there were lots of old rides - not as fast as they are now.

We always looked forward to the fair. There were relations who perhaps you hadn't seen for a year, but they'd come back for the fair. Granny had The White Hart pub and she always had a big ham in the back and the pub looked different to today's pubs – the barrels would all be set up in the bars and she'd draw beer from the barrels and during the fair there would be people spilling out into the street and you wouldn't have seen them all year. It was a real meeting point.

The fair was lit by naphtha flares. I suppose it was dangerous, but the fair doesn't seem the same to me now. And I liked to listen to the hurdy gurdy, and with all the steam engines it had a smell of its own. We had a few pennies to spend at the fair – we'd earn them by gleaning or helping Dad pick up the potatoes. We went on the roundabouts and bought rock. We had confetti and saw-dust balls covered in tinsel.

Baldock Fair used to be ankle-deep in confetti. It was sold for 1d a bag and you'd get hold of each other and tuck it down. We used to have to undress in the shed. Mum wouldn't let us in the house. We looked forward to the fair, but we never had much money but I remember my brother gave me and my sister a penny between us, so we bought some red rock from the Rock King. He used to auction all his rock off late at night. You could get sausages, fish and chips and whelks all down the bottom end near the Rock King.

The annual fair in the High Street with steam-driven rides and showmen's caravans.

The peaceful routine of daily life was dramatically shattered by the outbreak of war in 1914. Accommodation was needed for the men of the Cheshire Regiment who were billeted in the town and each house was inspected to see how many soldiers it could take. Refugees came from Belgium and many of the local young men went off to fight.

I remember in 1914 when I was a little lad seeing the train leave Baldock Station all bedecked in flags, with all the territorials and militia men leaving to go to the war. That was August 1914 and everybody made a fuss cheering, 'hurray, hurray,' – but half of 'em never came back.

When the First World War started, I can remember my father saying, 'The war's started – it's going to be terrible,' but I don't think anyone really knew how terrible it was. He went in for the last two years of the war, although he was over-age. During the whole war we had over 400 soldiers billeted on us. The war started on August 4th and by August 6th we had 10 soldiers staying with us! On August 6th the police just came round and asked to look over the house and see how many spare bedrooms we had. Well, we had four spare bedrooms so they said, 'Right, you can take 10 soldiers,' and that was that.

Very nice, some of those soldiers, Mother didn't have to feed them, just give them a bed for the night. She got four pence a day. I think she did give them odd bits to eat, though. They were the Cheshires; for years we had a picture of one of them, in his red tunic with broad white stripes and a big pink rosette.

Charles Wilsher, Royal Horse Artillery.

One of them was called Samuel, a real dapper little man, and when he thought they were going to France in about a fortnight's time, he said, 'I really must have some more money, I can't go to France with what I've got.' So my Father says, 'What are you going to do then?' 'Well, I shall write to my uncle and ask him for some money,' he says. So he does that, and in a few days back comes the money, twenty pounds! 'Well,' he said, 'you see, my uncle, he's Lord Samuel, you know!' He was something to do with the government at that time.

There was another one, he was with my mother about two days before they were due to go to France and he was watching my mother doing the mangling – with one of those big old-fashioned mangles. He said, 'If I put my fingers in the rollers, would you turn the handle?' She said, 'If you dare to put your fingers there, I'll turn the handle all right.' She said her heart was thumping at the thought of having to do it, but I bet she would have done it. You see he was frightened, he was only a young lad.

Later on there was Mr Boyce, he'd been in the trenches and he'd been gassed, terrible that was. And another one, he was a little lamp-lighter. And another one said he used to make artificial pips for Tickler's raspberry jam!

7th Battalion, Cheshire Regiment, drawn up in the High Street 1915.

A troop of cavalry riding down Whitehorse Street.

Baldock Volunteers, who were equivalent to the Home Guard in the Second World War.

There was one little tiny chap – he'd got a heavy moustache and he came from Macclesfield and his name was Basford and he said if he ever came out of the war, he would send us little girls some real silk handkerchiefs. Well I should think it was about 18 months after the end of the war that a flat box arrived, and Mum opened it and inside were a dozen of the most beautiful pure silk Macclesfield handkerchiefs that he'd sent us. He made us laugh about how many times he'd been to prison. Me mother said, 'Oh dear, have I got a prisoner?' and he said, 'It's all right, missus, it's only for poaching – I've never done anything worse than poaching – but I'm the biggest poacher in Macclesfield.' He'd been to prison dozens of times. They were lovely heavy silk handkerchiefs – they washed lovely.

And we had South Africans and two Scotch chappies – despatch riders they were – and they'd send their laundry home to Scotland every week to their mothers to wash. We rather liked that because when it came back there was cakes and sweets and peppermints in it which they used to dish out to us kids, so we didn't mind how long they stayed.

We had several South Africans – they were charming lads, all very young. And a lot of them died in that terrible flu. My father couldn't bury them quick enough it was a terrible epidemic.

There were lots of Australian and South African troops in the

Men of the Cheshire Regiment practising signalling in a field on the edge of the town, joined by a little boy on the right.

town. There was a severe blizzard and snow storm one year and the South African troops were so overwhelmed by the sight of snow that they built a giant snowman in the High Street and it was there for weeks.

Coal was rationed during the First World War. That was one of the biggest hardships because we cooked by it, too. We used to have to go down and queue at the gas works for half-a-hundredweight of coke – we'd queue there nearly all morning on a Saturday. Vegetables got short at the end of the war – things weren't rationed to the extent they were in the Second World War – we got short of things though – like tea. Father didn't have an allotment. I don't think he were capable of anything other than reading the bible. Mother used to get annoyed with him because she was a farmer's daughter.

And the Cheshire Regiment stayed here – they came and went – we had a couple with us – man and wife. Their headquarters was in Pepper Court and they were all in Elmwood Park under canvas.

And we had prisoners-of-war and there was some anti-German feeling against the Hergerts and when war broke out everyone was out in the streets making a noise and old Mrs Hergert came to the door and someone wrapped her in a Union Jack – terrible it was.

We didn't have the blackout in the First World War like we did in the second – but there wasn't the bright lights then. We only had a couple of oil lamps so there was no danger of going into a room and switching the electric light on.

I can see the prisoners-of-war coming from the station, swarms of them. They went up to Icknield Way East to the maltings on the Royston Road and our lot weren't too strict, they was free and easy with them. Not like the Germans were with us. Four of them had a pony and trap and they used to go by us in Icknield Way to work for Ben Parker at Norton. They was always whistling and my mum used to hear them and she'd say, 'Come on, time to get up, there's the Germans going to work.' They didn't get locked up. They used to walk around Baldock – they had patches on their clothes and wore a little round cap with a button on the front.

I remember the Cheshire Regiment staying in the town. They all went to the Dardanelles – they were lucky to come back. Two came back to marry Baldock girls. The Belgians lived in the mansion (Elmwood Manor) before it was burnt down. The soldiers were in there, too, and the Brewery House. Soldiers were also billeted in Bury House where there's a big bay window. That was their dining room and they'd have the window up and us little old kids would go and look at them and they'd shy lumps of sugar at us through the window.

I remember the Belgian refugees. They had a meat shop near where Philpotts is selling horse flesh for the Belgians and we'd see these carcasses of horses hanging up. They used to work at the Kryn and Lahy making munitions. There was no end of them. They nearly all went back after the war – one or two stopped behind, but mostly they went. They did say the Kryn and Lahy was built by the Belgians to make the munitions.

Booths had a girl there to translate for the Belgian refugees who came into the shop. Auntie Min who worked there knew that two of these refugees didn't want to go home after the war and she pleaded with Mum to take them in. Mum didn't really want any more boarders but she said all right. So we had them – Paul and René their names were and they had their own bedroom and sitting room. Well, the first morning, Mum says to Dad , 'What'll I give them to eat, I don't know what Belgians eat.' So he says, 'I should give them a beefsteak pudding.' So she made this pudding, put a cloth on the table, then came back with the pudding. Well, they'd taken the cloth off – they obviously weren't used to that, so she says, 'Come on, let's have that cloth back.' She puts the cloth back and goes away, but nothing seems to happen. So she says to Dad, 'They are not going to eat that,' when one of them comes through and says, 'Sauce!' She takes a bottle of HP sauce in and puts it on the table. She still can't hear anything so she goes in and they haven't touched it. She asks what's wrong and they just say 'sauce' again. She realises they mean gravy, and cuts them a big

Young soldiers of the Cheshire Regiment with members of the Cross family outside their shop.

piece each to show them the gravy's inside. Well that was all right and they ate it.

The next morning as they were going off to work she says to them, 'What do you want for tea tonight?' And they replied, 'Meat pudding.' And do you know, she made the same meal – meat pudding, mashed potatoes and Brussels sprouts – for a fortnight, until she said to my father, 'I can't make another pudding I've done it for a fortnight!'

The Catholic priest used to come and play cards with them and they used to have long clay pipes they used to smoke. Father Durein used to go around our churchyard with his prayer book muttering, because he didn't have a churchyard of his own and Dad came in one day and says, 'I've just had an omen. I came

Above: Fancy dress line-up for the Peace Parade 1919.
Centre: Procession in Whitehorse Street with the horse-drawn
fire-engine leading the floats.
Below: Walkers in the procession.

Above: Men who had served in the 1914-18 war, some still in uniform
Below: Allies and Empire float passing The Grange in the High Street.

through the churchyard and I've seen Father Durein in there in his long black gown and there's a horse running today called 'Black Gown'. I think I'll back it.' So he put £1 on it and it came in at 20–1.

The food situation was much worse in the First World War than in the Second World War. There were no coupons or anything until right at the end, so you just had to stand in queues and hope for the best. 'Have you a jar of treacle? Half a jar? Two ounces of tea?' Things like that. There was no system, so it was just a matter of first come, first served. I think meat was scarcer in the Second World War, though, because in the First War most of the butchers killed their own meat.

I was a paper boy in Baldock during the First World War and one thing I remember particularly – there was a blizzard and I'd been round with the papers at night, and all in the High Street, up the right side where Tesco's is, there were big trees and they all laid up the High Street in the road. It was several weeks before the soldiers could saw them up and let the traffic go by.

At the end of the First World War I remember a Zeppelin came over and broke into two and Dad, being a fireman, got all his gear on and went over and he said it was terrible, you could see the imprint in the earth where the bodies landed after jumping out of this airship.

Me and my sister took part in the Peace Procession, she was only four and I was five and we were done up as costers pushing a little barrow. Then at night there was this huge bonfire outside what is now the Goldcrest Hotel.

I don't think life was ever the same again after the First World War, it altered people. You see, our father's generation had all been in the war and that altered people's outlook completely, especially those that had been on active service and they'd seen such a different world outside Baldock.

Changing with the Times
1920s to 1945

The destruction of Elmwood Manor was to be more significant than anyone imagined. It stood derelict for about three years, but then a proposal to build a factory on the site came from Kosmos, a photographic processing firm from Letchworth. Before the building was occupied, they ran into financial difficulties, and eventually the Full-Fashioned Hosiery Company took over.

I remember seeing the shell of Elmwood Manor standing there for years. Then they took the fence away and the elm trees came down and they started building. The architect used to come and park his car by our window – a green Daimler tourer with two big red seats in the back and he'd go to the George and Dragon for his lunch. But apparently there wasn't enough money to finish the building.

I can remember the Bondor being built when I was at school, probably about 1919/20. My father went and worked there and they built a replica of that building – it was white – and they used to take it to the White City in the back of a lorry. The people who built the original factory went bankrupt and then a consortium of about six people from Halifax-way started the Full-Fashioned Hosiery Company and later, when John Goodenday got involved, it became the Bondor. Then it got affiliated to some place in America and became Kayser Bondor. Some people say this was when all the gentry started to leave the town, but I don't think so, I think they got older, their families grew up and they just dispersed. I think it made the town, because there was nothing here but the brewery until then. It opened up employment for all the young people.

The Bondor was built as the Kosmos Photographics at first, but the family went broke and it stood empty for years. The brickwork is very good. All the bricks were carried from Baldock Station by horse and cart to build it.

The Full-Fashioned Hosiery Company, early 1920s.

The Full-Fashioned Hosiery Company then took the building

Mansfield Road (formerly New Road — see p.25), with its newly-built houses for the Bondor workers coming from the Midlands.

over and brought people from the Midlands. They earned four or five times more money than we did. All the houses up Mansfield Road were built for them.

I remember all the people coming from Mansfield and all those houses being built on that lovely park – Elmwood Park. It brought a lot of employment to the town, but I often wonder what would have happened if Elmwood Manor hadn't burnt down and that factory had never been built. Perhaps Baldock might still have been a quiet little country town?

Apart from the new factory in 'The Park', the town didn't change dramatically in the inter-war years. More motorised traffic was seen, but many tradesmen still delivered by horse and cart. And daily life was brightened by a few individuals who didn't always conform with the accepted way of living.

We had better shopping facilities in the 20s than what we have today – in my opinion Baldock progressed backwards.

In Whitehorse Street there was a little shop – tiny shop it was – kept by Mrs Ellis, and she sold cottons and things like that. Then there was Butlers on the other side of the road selling bicycles, Oliver Charter the saddler, Worbeys the Butcher, and Wilsons. Then there was Farrs, Bishops, Booths, then The Rose and Crown, a barber's shop, and Mrs Stamford in the sweetshop.

The nice smells have disappeared from Baldock – the first smell you got in Whitehorse Street was the malt from the maltings, then the smell of bread from Farr's bakery and on the opposite side of the road there were herbs drying up Womback Yard. Then turn into the High Street and you could smell the hops at the brewery; then there was Hanscombes selling their bread, Juffs bakers in Hitchin street and Mr Barker down Church Street.

Mrs Stamford sold sweets from her little shop on the corner of the High Street. We used to have a penny or ha'penny to spend and we'd go in and stand on the chair in her shop because we were so small then, so that we could have a good look round to see what to spend our ha'penny on. Then there was another sweet shop in a dirty little house at the bottom of Church Street – but we weren't allowed to go in there! They were little slums down there, terrible places. Then there was another shop in one of the Ten Houses (Prospect Terrace) in Clothall Road. Mr Bowskill used to sell sweets and make ice cream in the summer and faggots in the winter.

A man would come round selling fish from a cart, shouting out down the street, 'Yarmouth kippers, bloaters' and everyone would come out of their houses and buy their herrings, kippers or whatever. And the muffin man would come round the streets in winter, with his bell.

There were shops for everybody's needs in Baldock in those days. There was a jewellers, Mr Bate's; Mr Newling's clothing shop; Mr Jones sold wet fish and opened the first milk bar in the town; Oliver Charter's shop sold everything made of leather and so on; two men's clothing shops, Wilsons and Dysons. Then there was Booth's Stores, well you could get everything there, men's clothing, ladieswear, children's clothes, shoes, hosiery, bedding, materials, curtaining, even carpets and lino. The children used to like to watch the cash system, because it was like a little overhead railway. You put the money in a container and pulled a handle and it shot along the wires to the cash desk where Mrs Booth would work out the bill and then send back the change. Sometimes she'd get it wrong and you'd have to send it back, but she was lovely was Mrs Booth. And sometimes the container would get stuck half-way down the shop and then you'd have to go and give it a prod.

At Booths we sold artificial silk stockings at 1/11¾d and pure silk stockings at 2/11d. Lisle stockings were expensive, half-a-crown a pair but we did do cheaper ones in the sales at a shilling a

Bate's, the jewellers, no.2 High Street.

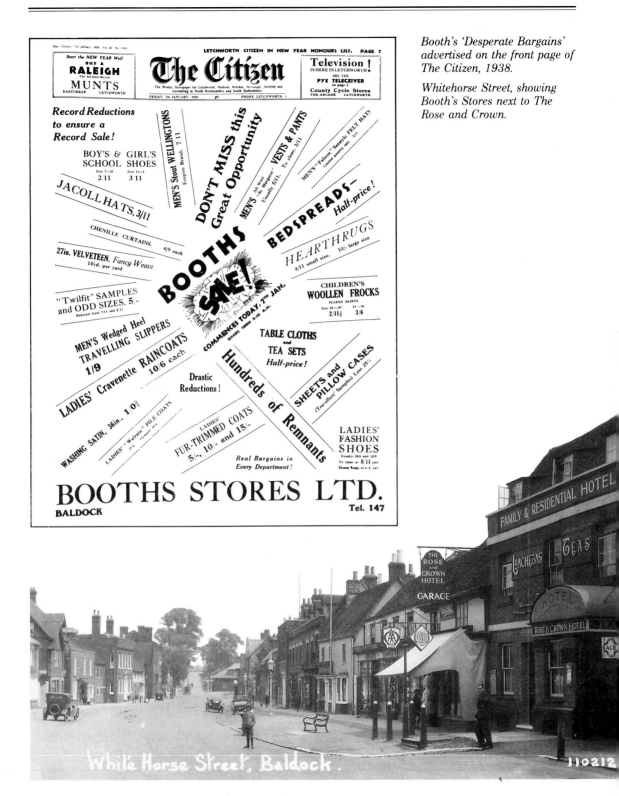

Booth's 'Desperate Bargains' advertised on the front page of The Citizen, 1938.

Whitehorse Street, showing Booth's Stores next to The Rose and Crown.

pair. They were awful things, only came up just above the knee.

Then we sold cretonne at 1/0¾d a yard and this plain dress material at 4½d that's 2p a yard! We had it all piled up outside the shop with a big price ticket on it and we sold no end of that. Then once we even had some in at 2¾d a yard. It was very stiff but when you washed it, all the dressing came out and it went completely limp.

Wool was 5d an ounce, lino 1/11d a square yard and you could get a good pair of sheets for 12/11d and pillowcases for about 1/6d a pair.

We always used to have a sale each year – 'Desperate Bargains', Derek used to call them. People used to queue up outside and we'd call out, 'Are you all ready?' then we'd open the doors and get behind the counters and the people would come tearing in, all wanting the things out of the windows. 'I want this! I want that!' We'd never know who'd asked first for things – we used to hate those sales!

But they were happy times. . . .

One of the highlights was when the fire-engine went out. The bell used to ring and everybody stopped what they were doing and ran to the corner of the street to wait to see the engine go. This was the Merryweather, kept in the Fire Station which was part of the Town Hall. It had Baldock Fire Station carved in stone over the doors. The firemen would come rushing up and a lot of them could drive, so whoever got there first, he climbed in the driver's seat and was allowed to be the driver for the day.

I remember the smell of lime trees on very hot summer days as you came down the High Street – this was in the early 20s when there were only about three cars in Baldock – just horses and carts. We'd stop at the brewery and watch the horses and carts

Baldock's first motor fire engine, 1922, made by Merryweather.

Whitehorse Street, 1928.

unload there and see the bags of grain being drawn up the outside of the building. There were nursemaids from all the big houses with their retinue of children and the nurse and the undernurse – from Sir Benjamin Cherry at The Grange. The Manor House was Dr Watson's, South Lodge was Terence Eden, Pepper Court was the Convent School – I went to school there. Holford House was Captain and Mrs Morgan, the Brewery House was Miss Cotton-Brown and the Czech House (13 Whitehorse Street) was Miss Saville.

Mrs de Bathe lived down Hitchin Street and Mrs Serocold at St Mary's House. There was the Band of Hope down the old Congregational Church – you weren't allowed to drink if you belonged to that. Mr Izzard, who lived in Pembroke Road, used to run that – there used to be little concerts, I went to the Church – Sunday School in the mornings and church in the afternoon.

I remember King George V and Queen Mary coming through to go to the races at Newmarket and you always used to line up at the side of the road if you knew the king was coming.

We lived in a cottage near The Compasses and many times cars would lose things out of their 'dicky' seats as they came down that bumpy road into Baldock from Biggleswade. My father picked up fishing rods and sets of golf clubs and all sorts. He took them into the Police Station but they were never claimed, I suppose the cars made a lot of noise and they wouldn't know whereabouts on the

Rear of Butler's Garage with the result of one of the 'spectacular crashes'.

road they'd lost them. Anyway he always got them back after so many weeks and he usually used them to pay the doctors' bills with – I should think the doctors did rather well out of it.

The doctors ran a club, the Sick Club, for the townspeople and you paid in your pennies, or whatever, each week and then that put you on that doctor's 'panel', and if you were ill then he'd come and visit because a doctor's visit was expensive then, usually about 7/6 I think.

We used to have some spectacular crashes in those days. Once a load of strawberries went over on the Royston Road and all the local kids helped clear them up! Another time a load of tea went over by the Astonia Cinema, to *everybody's* benefit!

We all lived in the house at the bottom of Limekiln Lane in South Road. In the front was a long shed which housed a huge wringer machine which was worked by a large wheel, as big as a cartwheel. All the people in the road used to use it. At the side of the house were two thatched cottages. At the back was a well where we got our water, and a huge orchard ran up to half the length of the Lane. Where the caravan site is now, there was once a riding school.

Over the road facing us, was a farm and we used to run through a little lane, known as Juffs Lane, to Juffs' shop to get our sweets or bits of groceries. On the side of the farm were six houses which are still there, and at the end there was one on its own. An old lady named Mrs Elsom lived there. She used to frighten me by saying that, in a thunderstorm, we should cover mirrors up, hide the cutlery and sit away from windows.

On our side of the road there were no houses, but there was a fruit and flower garden run by a Mr Peters. It always smelt so fragrant. From there to Clothall Road roundabout, it was fields,

Juffs' van, outside the bakery in Pinnocks Lane.

Below: The Riding School, Limeliln Lane.

except at the very end were there was a house owned by Mr Booth. Opposite there was Dean's engineering business. Going down Clothall Road were the ten houses, and next to them was a big field called Dean's Meadow. It now has about 30 private houses which end at Pinnocks Lane next to Pembroke Road. Half-way down this road, where Miss Bate lived, was a little ironmongers shop called Izzards. He used to go round calling out, 'Any ale today,' meaning oil. His wife was tossed by a bull in Clarke's Lane while walking her dog. He sold brooms for 6d.

I can remember South Road when it was just a track, Weston Way when it was an archway of trees, no houses at that time, the surrounding park of the Manor House where we used to gather violets, primroses etc., so quiet and peaceful — no fear of racing traffic when crossing the road, and those little cottages past the Studio Café and The Compasses public house.

There were four maltings in Baldock. There was one in Royston Road, there was one up near Hanscombes, one where they sell cars – Roes Maltings – the one that Geary's had and turned into a furniture shop (they belonged to Paynes) and the one on the corner of Clothall Road, that was Simpsons. They made all their own malt for their beer and stout. Stout was a bit tricky to make because there was a fire risk and the barley had to be absolutely black. They had to be ever so careful as they had to create more heat. Albert Emery was the maltster there and he was an expert at it. I watched them when I was a lad.

We came to Baldock in 1923. My parents were going to keep the Black Eagle in Baldock. We were in the thick of it there. That was the rough end – there were always scraps in the pub.

Beer was 4d a pint so there were plenty of fights. Mother and father kept the pub; mother ran it during the day because my father went to work – I was only nine when we came. It was a Wells and Winch pub. If you sold a barrel you earned £1 and that had to cover lighting and heating and your living.

There was a fight nearly every day. They used to drink Friday, Saturday and Sunday and then they had no money for the rest of the week. There was darts, dominoes and ring-a-ball; they'd play for a packet of Woodbines, and we ran a football sweep and had a supper at the end of the season – that was a good evening. We

One of the courts leading off Church Street.

Many cottages were demolished in the 1920s, particularly in Norton End (see p.22).

took 1d off people during the year and we'd put on ham, beef, cheese rolls and pickles in the open at the back of the pub and beer flowed freely. It was marvellous – we always seemed to have a fine evening. We had a dish of beef from Chapmans, they cut it up into slices.

The only food we served at other times was bread and cheese and an onion for 2d – they used to have half-a-pint and bread and cheese for 4d. Some were a bit happy by the time they went home. In those days if you had four pints of bitter which cost 7d a pint, your old legs would go. Nowadays, you could stand there all night drinking and it would only make you run.

The draymen brought the barrels in – we only had to tap them. I used to help me dad – he'd give me half-a-pint of beer and one Woodbine – that was my pay.

We didn't call the police if there was trouble, we just pitched them out. A policeman used to come around about a minute before closing time and you couldn't finish your beer, you just had to get out. We also used to have the Salvation Army come round with the War Cry on a Saturday night. They used to meet in Football Close where Rusbridge's garage now is.

At Christmastime we had a Guess-the-Seeds-in-the-Marrow competition; to make it interesting, a tin of biscuits or some beer was the prize.

We used to put decorations up and every customer who came in

The Manor House in the High Street with railings and elegant gate pillars intact c.1920.

Moss's grocer's shop with gaslit window display for Christmas.

in the morning got a free pint – perhaps between 12 and 1. Women didn't go into pubs much then – we didn't have a spirit licence, so we could only serve beer and ginger wine. People used to bring a jug or bottle and if a child came to get some for its parents you had to put a seal on the bottle.

We went to chapel and I can remember the curfew ringing round about half-past-six every night. Johnny Cawdell rang it, and right up to the war the death knell rang when anyone died. The last war took out many customs – we used to have Baldock doughnuts. Mr Barker, the baker down Church Street, used to have a big notice in his window on Ash Wednesday saying, 'Doughnut Day'. They used to be small nuts of dough, no jam in them, just spiced dough. You used to be able to get a small oblong cake with a few sultanas in it and I used to run to the baker's to get it warm.

Although it was a fairly rough end of town, near the Black Eagle, you weren't afraid of being attacked or anything like that. Even the gypsies were all right. They used to camp along the highway – there was no trouble – we only had the odd scrap if anyone had had too much to drink, but it was only a bit of fun. If you knocked a bloke down, you'd let him get up again, you wouldn't put the boot in. We'd just have a bit of fun – we'd get a black eye and someone would say, 'Coo, that's a beauty,' and that was it.

The Library used to be in the Town Hall, and at another time in a room in what is now the Goldcrest Hotel. It did move about a bit before coming to rest in Bell Row. The entrance was in Hitchin

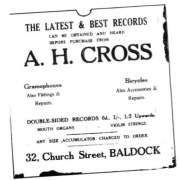

BOOKING OFFIC. COACHES TEL 82

Allnutt's Templar Ca

CAFE

CREAM ICE

Allnutt's cafe in the High Street, advertising soda fountains and cream ices.

Street where the Museum's Natural History Department was until recently. Mr Stevenson was in charge, but the staff were all volunteers with the books being supplied by Herts. County Council, who changed the entire stock once a year. I helped in the Children's Library when I was about 12 to 14 years old. You were only allowed to choose two books a week, one fiction and one non-fiction, and you had to do it in strict silence, you only had to breathe too heavily and you'd be 'shushed' by Mr Stevenson.

I didn't like the girls' stories, no Angela Brazil for me, although girls' school stories were popular, I preferred to read my brother's adventure books by G A Henty.

Mr Lionel Jones ran what was known as the 'Tramps Library' from an old stables at the end of Hitchin Street in part of what was the sport's shop that has recently closed down. He was a retired gentleman and he had a great regard for those he called 'Knights of the Road', and at that time there were a lot of men tramping round looking for work, quite a lot of whom had been in the First World War.

Anyway he begged and borrowed lots of books until he'd got quite a little library and then he put up bookshelves all round this little room and sat in there all day and these men knew there was somewhere where they could always call in. They could have a sit down and a read there, or if they wanted to borrow a book, Mr Jones would probably let them. He was a really nice old gentleman and he had plenty of leisure time so he probably enjoyed having a talk with them, because a lot of them were quite educated men.

Mr Jones lived with his brother and sister next door but one to us, in a quiet little household all together. His brother, Hussey, would sleep out in the front garden in the summertime. I can remember looking out of my bedroom window and seeing him stretched out on his camp bed under the trees.

There were so many men tramping the roads in those days during the 20s. A lot of them had been in the war and when it was over found there was no one or no job to come back to and others had had such a terrible war and had been so unsettled, mentally, that they really couldn't fit into a job properly. So many of them were well educated, repectable men, too. They'd come to the door asking for a drop of water to make their tea and my mother always gave them a mug of cocoa and probably bread and cheese or a bit of cake.

Sometimes, if a man turned up late in the evening asking for a drink or asking if we knew of somewhere he could sleep, my mother would say he could sleep in the kitchen by the stove and she never locked the doors or anything. Nothing was ever taken, well only once, but usually they'd ask if they could chop any firewood or dig a bit of garden for you and they'd do it and be off early the next morning, before we got up sometimes.

By the late 20s several of the big houses were empty, well, times were hard and there had been several 'crashes' on the stock exchange. The Wilderness was empty all through my childhood and so was The Grange as Sir Benjamin Cherry had gone bankrupt. I can remember looking through the letter box of The Grange and seeing all the dried leaves going swirling up the flagstoned hall, in the draught from the open letter box, I suppose. Dr Watson lived in the Manor House at first, but then that stood empty for quite a time until Mr and Mrs O'Brien moved in just before the war. Cambridge House had been a college, but then Mrs de Bathe came to live there, wife of Captain de Bathe, Anglo-Irish I think, but the Captain had 'Reported to Glory', as they say, by then. Then Grove House was the school of course, mainly for daughters of farmers and more well-to-do tradesmen, they took boarders there too. You'd see the girls out walking in a 'crocodile', either to church or to take the fresh air round the town.

Pepper Court was the convent school and then there was St Joseph's Convent, too, but that had more refugees in during the war, mainly ladies. Then 13 Whitehorse Street, the big Georgian house, that was where Mrs Saville lived and then later on Mrs Kefford, who took in the Welsh girls and then later it became known as the Czech House, because of the Czech refugees who came here in 1938 at the time of the German invasion of Czechoslovakia – Munich and Chamberlain and all that.

The town looked cleaner in the 20s and 30s than it does now; we only had old John Cawdell who went round with his barrow and his brush and shovel, but he kept it nice and clean. I've always liked Baldock, I think it's a nice place to be, friendly, happy and at one time I could name everybody who lived both sides of every road.

Above: Pupils of Grove House private school in Whitehorse Street.

The re-opening of the market, 1925, with Jimmy Temple, the Town Crier, in his top hat.

The character that used to amuse me when I was a lad, was the Town Crier. He used to deck up in his clothes and he was the landlord of The Victoria pub – Jimmy Temple. He'd come round ringing that bell and shouting out what was going to happen and what wasn't going to happen.

There was the chimney sweep – old Tommy Barcock, he was a character. He'd go off for a ride on a Sunday afternoon in his pony and trap around the countryside and Mrs Barcock would sit up beside him, so sedate, round Weston and Clothall. All those bags of soot used to be packed along Orchard Road; he was a good sweep.

Mrs Lloyd who was married to the headmaster lived on the corner of Templar Avenue. She was a real school-teacher type and she says, 'Now I want to see that brush come out the top.' Anyway, whatever happened, the chimney pot came off and it fell down right through their conservatory. So Tommy says to her, 'Well the brush came out the top, didn't it?'

He was a town institution; I don't know how he came to lose his hand – he had a hook. He used to charge a shilling to sweep a chimney and he'd arrive in his pony and cart, with his little black dog beside him – and he used to swear! Swearing was terrible in

Tommy Barcock, the chimney sweep, and friends out for a drive in his pony and trap.

The AA scout who directed the traffic at the cross roads when King George V drove through Baldock to the races at Newmarket.

those days but he used to swear! I used to dread his yearly visitations, as we had to eat breakfast in the kitchen, it had a table but only a cold stone floor. Everything had to be covered up you see, he made such a mess, soot everywhere! He'd send us children out into the garden to see if the brush had come out of the top of the chimney, and then he had to have his cup of tea and a slice of my mother's cake. He never washed before he had it, oh no, he must have had as much soot inside as out, I should think.

I remember Totty Rayner – she used to frighten me to death. She lived round Pembroke Road – always had an umbrella up and wore black, but when she spoke she had a lovely voice, well-educated she was, but she was crossed in love, I believe. I remember hearing her speak one day up near the Station – she asked someone if they'd seen a grey-haired man. Whether she had a man on her mind I don't know – a man as let her down maybe.

Then there were the Smythes – they were three nice ladies. They did everything for the church and Sunday School. They worked all the year round for the children's Sunday School treat and Christmas Party. Mary died first and the other two were knocked down in Mansfield Road – it was terribly sad. I heard they were never allowed to get married. The tale went that one of them did have a boyfriend but the father said he would cut them out of everything if they got married, but that's hearsay.

William Sale, farmer, born 1845, died 1949. It is said that at one time his family owned land which stretched from Baldock to Buntingford.

Then there was Miss Sale. I used to get on with her, she taught me at Sunday School. She invited my mum and me up to tea in Letchworth Road — she was getting on and she said something about, 'When I'm not here,' and I said, 'Don't talk like that, Baldock wouldn't go on without you,' and she said, 'Ooh, you are lovely, fancy saying a thing like that.' I liked her but a lot of people didn't. She had a hard life. She was another one who wasn't allowed to get married – that was her uncle. He was afraid of the land going out of the family.

There used to be some black sheds on the way to Clothall where the tramps used to sleep. One old lady got drunk on meths in the town and PC Brett tried to arrest her, so she threw her arms round his neck and wrapped her legs around him so that he couldn't move. He didn't know what to do but he got her off and sent her on her way.

Then there was the policeman, Mr Dunk, who grew those great big pumpkins and he'd put them in a wheelbarrow and come and put them in Patterson's window. It was for some newspaper competition. They were huge things – they filled the wheelbarrow. He was strict, but there was no vandalism. You might scrump the odd apple. We used to go round old Miss Storey's when she went up Baldock Fair and we'd scrump her apples.

I remember Bertie Clements but no, he weren't all that eccentric, he knew what he was doing. Bert Clements got a living where a lot of people wouldn't. He used to go and get whatever was available in the countryside and he'd take it to Ransoms and he got a living that way. He was marvellous at picking poppies. I've seen him up the fair dancing on the Whip. He used to share it with Charlie Scoot. It wasn't ballroom dancing, I don't know what you'd call it. They used to do a bit of dancing in front of the organ at the fair. They were quite good, they could do high kicks.

Bertie Clements used to have a little sweet shop near the Church School – it was in an old thatched cottage there in Park Street. He always dressed as a woman – and you went down a big step into his shop and it was very dark in there. We'd buy gobstoppers and liquorice – if we had a ha'penny or penny or we'd go round to Hanscombes for vinegar flat or buns at dinner-time.

On Horticultural Show day there was always a fancy dress parade through the town and Bertie Clements would dance in this procession, made up. He was quite a character – he appeared at all the pubs and clubs.

Bertie Clements lived near us. He was a hard worker. He collected herbs and things and made a fortune out of it and had two bungalows built – they're still up Salisbury Road.

Johnny Booth lived in South Road and he had a grocer's shop

Cooper's Christmas display, High Street, 1925.

and mixed meat and all sorts and had a slaughter house up Clothall Road. He was a character. He was Chairman of the Magistrates and he used to leave his cart outside the Town Hall with his supplies and potatoes, go to court, try the blokes what had done wrong, then come out and ply his trade again.

I remember Teddy Cooper with his meat shop, cutting up the carcasses outside the shop. He used to skin sheep in Trusslers Yard and there was a hand-pump and a well in Pond Lane. He'd skin them and then open them, then wash it all down afterwards. Other animals were killed there, too.

Teddy Cooper had a high-class butcher's shop. At Christmastime all the carcasses were paraded and he had a beast hanging up outside with a notice on it saying, 'This beast was fed by Colonel Pryor at Weston', and old Johnny Booth opposite had a pig hanging up outside his shop with a notice on it saying, 'This pig fed itself'.

Although many married women had done war-work in the First World War, it was still more common for women to confine themselves to household chores once they married. And when children came along, looking after the house was a full-time occupation. Washing machines and vacuum cleaners were now

Opposite, above: Cottage garden in California 1932.

Opposite, below: Clarke's Yard at the bottom end of Church Street, photographed at about the same time as the picture above.

available, but these were not for the 'ordinary' people who continued to light the copper on a Monday morning just as their mothers had done, and struggled to make the housekeeping go as far as possible.

At home we had the copper in the corner of the kitchen for heating the water. You'd burn all your old rubbish under the copper, old shoes, anything. You'd do the washing in the copper, and then put it through the mangle. We cooked on the kitchen range – no gas – and had our baths in front of the range, lovely that was! Friday night was bath night, with the water heated up in the copper again. We used it at Christmas for boiling the puddings, you could do half-a-dozen at once in it, which saved all that messing about with saucepans. Useful things those coppers were.

We lived on one of the County Council's smallholdings along the Buntingford Road. Although built after the First World War, they only had the mains water supply laid on, so cooking was done on a range and if you didn't want to wash in cold water you had to boil a kettle, and light the copper for washing clothes. Our only lighting was by Aladdin oil lamps which you had to pump up, and my father had an old carbide lamp as well. It gave a lovely bright light, but smelt of rotten eggs! When you went up to bed you took a candle with you, and as there was no heating upstairs, it was like an ice-box in winter with the north wind blowing straight across the fields. Having no electricity, we had an 'accumulator' for the wireless set – a heavy, square, glass, wet-battery that we had to get recharged every week or so at Mr Izzard's shop in Pembroke Road. We lived with this until electricity finally came in 1947, but we had to pay to have it laid on.

Of course, there was no mains drainage so we had an earth closet out at the back and later on an Elsan which was a bit more

Haymaking in the fields on Weston Way.

Pinnocks Lane. The field behind the hedge on the left was used for grazing horses.

modern. I used to visit friends in Baldock and think how nice it was just to pull a chain! I know that my mother was always embarrassed at having to explain to visitors about that closet.

Farm work was hard in those days and everyone worked long hours. When I was a child we had horses for ploughing and carting and I was driving a horse and cart when I was 14. We kept cows, which were milked by hand twice a day, and twice a day we had to clean the milk cooler with boiling water and scrub out the dairy with a hand broom and see to the milk churns and so on. The cows came into the milking shed three at a time for milking, which my father usually did, then the first three would amble out and the next three came in. I remember one cow, Dolly, we had for 20 years, and a little hand-reared piglet, the runt of the litter, called Henry, who grew into an enormous boar with great big tusks. He was always all right with me, but I never took any chances, when I fed him it was with a bucket in one hand and a pitchfork in the other!

Of course, the animals always came first, they were our livelihood after all. They had their breakfast, then we had ours. After lunch on Christmas afternoon we'd sit by the fire until about three, then it was time to go out and start seeing to the livestock so that we could be finished by seven o'clock and have the rest of Christmas Day to ourselves.

My mother was a good and inventive cook, she made her own bread and cakes, of course, and jam. We grew our own vegetables and everything came in its season. Rabbits were very cheap and were eaten a lot, they were field rabbits so you had to look out for lead shot whilst you were eating them.

Then mother was very partial to bloaters, she'd impale one on the toasting fork and we had a kitchen range with a ledge in front of the fire, and she'd put it in a tin on that and sit in front of the fire. Mother loved bloaters, but Father wanted kippers and I wouldn't have either!

Whether children liked or loathed school depended largely on the teachers. Some were universally disliked, while others made lessons more bearable – and sometimes even enjoyable.

I started off in the Infants' School with Miss Taylor and Miss Christopher. I didn't like her because she thumped me in the back once for writing a letter the wrong way round. I wrote a letter 'e' backwards and she thumped me, I never did like her after that, but everybody else did, she was ever so popular. She'd get into trouble now if she did that sort of thing! Mrs Lawton was my friend! I never did know what I'd done, but she'd come up and rap you on the knuckles with a ruler. She was very fond of that ruler!

Then there was the school bell. It would start ringing at five-to-nine. We lived in Salisbury Road then and had to walk all that way to Park Street. Sometimes it would stop ringing long before we reached Pepper Alley and we were such little kids and Marge was carting us about and she'd say, 'Hurry up, it's ten-to-nine!' I never did know what 'ten-to-nine' meant but I knew it was dreadful! We'd have to run and I can remember being all out of breath and Miss Bridgeman used to be in the playground with her whistle . . . you'd have to creep in... they were ever so strict about you being late.

The water supply at The Nook Cottage, Great North Road, 1926.

A class at St Mary's Church School, Park Street, in the early 1930s.

We went home for lunch, there were no school dinners but we took our elevenses, a packet of sandwiches or something, bread and sugar, and we had to put them all in a basket in the classroom and then take them out at mid-morning break. You were also allowed to go to Hanscombes for a bun; one person was chosen, who'd take the money, a penny or whatever and they'd go and get the lovely hot buns.

In the mornings I was always late leaving home and if I wasn't careful, I'd catch the cows going out of New Farm to cross the road into the meadow where The Rowans is now. They used to go in a gate almost opposite the end of Chilvers Bank into this lovely lush meadow. I was always terrified of cows and if I was a minute or two late I had to stand and wait until they'd all gone in. I was always being late.

I went to the Church School to Lloyd's tender mercies, I didn't like it, I accepted it. I didn't like the cane and old Lloyd could certainly dish that out, he was a shocker!

London Road in the thirties
when traffic was light.

When I went to Hitchin Boys School I used to cycle; there were several of us, Olaf and I, Jack Bysouth, Sonny Waters, Mervyn Pratt, Nobby Clark. Mostly we went on our bikes, but sometimes we went on the train or on Dennis's bus from Ashwell, but we tended to make a bit of a nuisance of ourselves on the bus, so then we'd go back to the bikes. We'd wait for one of Simpson's Foden steam wagons from the brewery and then hang on the back, all six of us in a line sometimes – it was damn dangerous, but there. . . .

I went to Pond Lane School, Mr Hancock was headmaster and our teachers were Mrs Shaw, Miss Parkinson – she was the nicest – and Miss Henderson. I was sent for punishment by Mr Armstrong once, because he'd never smack anyone. And you had to go across this yard. So I went half way and stopped and came back, rubbing my arm and pretending to sniffle.

We had cooking with Miss Cater and she was nice, but we had to clear the cupboards out every so often and we got in there one time and found the currants which we started eating. Then we found some dough and we started shying little pieces up onto the ceiling – we didn't think we could be seen . . . but we did penance for that.

In the very cold winters – and they always seemed to be cold – I remember all the school children and the teachers at the Pond Lane School, before school started, would run from the school to the railway bridge and back to get warm. And during break-times we'd make a slide across the playground and slide up and down that, again to keep warm – teachers as well!

Walking home from school along Weston Way, particularly at lunchtime, we'd often meet a farm cart coming along, loaded with manure, and we'd run past holding our noses. It was great fun, too, when a bullock got loose in the town, trying to catch it as it ran down the alleyways off Icknield Way and Football Close. It didn't happen often, but I remember a few occasions when it did.

Motor traffic gradually increased through the twenties, and it was no longer possible for children to play on the main roads, so they moved into the side streets, hung around lamp-posts and found their friends from families who lived in the same area. They were still largely free spirits who could wander the fields and hills around without restriction.

As children we often played in the road, under the gas lamps until we were called into bed by our mothers. They did not have to worry in those days about child abduction and all the rest. Our chief anxiety was, I believe, fear of the bats that came swooping around on a summer evening, because it was said that if you got one in your hair you could never get it out!

There were no mod-cons in those days; we had an outside lava-

tory, as did most people, and the cold water tap was outside too. But no one seemed to worry about this. The bedrooms were often freezing in the winter, even if we were ill! We bathed in front of the kitchen fire where there was a huge kitchen-range and this was lovely in cold weather. We used a 'hip-bath' and later a 'bungalow' bath and managed to keep quite clean! On a cold or wet day we would sit, usually with our special friends, and cut up newspapers for the lav, which we then strung up and hung on the wall.

On Sundays we followed a very strict routine – Sunday School at the Congregational Church in Whitehorse Street and we usually had morning and afternoon sessions, apart from which we were

Pupils of St Mary's Infants' School in Park Street, 1925, with headmistress, Miss Christopher.

Headmaster, J V Lloyd, and pupils at the Park Street Church of England School, 1922.

only permitted to go for a walk or read. In the garden there were and still are apple trees, Bramley and two Blenheim Orange, and we were very popular among the children when harvest time came round. A gang would collect outside the garden gate and two of us would collect as many apples as we could without being seen by our strict great-aunts. We'd then carry them to the other children by putting the apples up our knicker-legs which were very capacious in those days, (perhaps having to be handed down in the family!) and grabbed with great jubilation by the gang waiting patiently outside. We loved to go up 'Chalky Lane' now know as Limekiln Lane, taking a picnic meal, and then on to the Weston Hills, where we spent many happy hours running down the hills, swinging on trees and rushing about the dead leaves in the wood. We had no regular pocket money, but were given the odd penny and it was amazing how much this would buy. We got gob-stoppers, Felix eyes, liquorice, something called 'tobacco' but tasting much better, sherbert dabs, vinegar flats etc.

I used to like locust beans, you'd get them in a ha'penny dip. You were supposed to get sweets wrapped up in coloured paper, but often it was broken bits of wafer biscuit, popcorn, stuff like that and locust (or carob) beans. They were black and sweet, about three inches long, a bit like a black slug and if you were lucky there was a *real diamond ring* as well!

I used to get sixpence a week pocket money which divided up into tuppence for the Guide subs, tuppence for the Guide Magazine and tuppence for the church collection – but if I was lucky I got a 'Tuesday penny' and that's where my sweets came from!

When I was very little and before pocket money started, I'd

A Sunday School outing with members and minister of the Congregational Church.

A summer afternoon in Avenue Field. An old tree trunk could provide hours of entertainment if you were young enough to see its possibilities.

sometimes get 'The Sunbeam' or 'Chicks' Own' bought for me.

I always found it hard to sleep in summertime and if I was awake at night, round about three o'clock in the morning, I would hear all the lorries coming through the town on their way to Covent Garden and then about six they'd all be coming back. The traffic was really heavy in those days through the town, all of these lorries would be bringing vegetables down to London from Bedfordshire and even Lincolnshire, being on the Great North Road.

Whips and tops and marbles were summer games, well, you couldn't play them in the wet, and marbles you'd play in the dust. Skipping was more all year round and hoops, too; boys had metal ones and girls had wooden ones. They were sold at toy shops but some of the boys' metal hoops were the hoops off the beer barrels and they guided them along with a metal stick with a hook. Then boys also had conkers, of course, and lots of them had go-carts, made of soap boxes and old pram wheels, but, of course, there's nowhere for them to go nowadays but then they could run all the way down the London Road or come down Royston Road.

I was in the Guides and our favourite site for a camp fire was in the old chalk pit up the Clothall Road. (It's not there now, it was on the left just as you go up the hill before the road sweeps down again to the Clothall turn-off.) It was a good steep pit, well sheltered from the wind so we could light our camp fire and have our 'cheese-fries', nightmares really! We all had to bring cheese sandwiches and some fat and someone provided the frying pan and we'd fry our sandwiches over the fire. The only trouble was that everybody brought something different, some people brought 'Trex', others lard or margarine, posh people brought butter, others dripping; anyway, in it all went, in one great mixture . . . no wonder most of us felt bad in the night afterwards!

There was a certain magic being out under the old gas lamps that you don't get from electric ones now. If we stayed out late enough, Mr Scoot would come round and pull a chain to turn the lamp on and then the boys would have a rope over the arm of the lamp standard and would be swinging round it, though they'd have to keep an eye open for PC Dunk. I remember one boy scrumping apples along the Twitchell, and came over the wall right into the arms of PC Dunk. 'Shall I tell your father or shall I box your ears?' The boy thought it would be hard to explain scrumping to his father (especially as he was a greengrocer!) so he opted for the boxed ears. He said his ears rang for days!

Mrs Timms who kept a shop down Church Street was a bit of a character. Her head hardly came up to the counter and we'd send her up this ladder for sweets and pinch something from the counter.

Theo Cox's father used to have fruit outside his shop and I remember the pomegranates being there and I used to say, 'Right, someone say go,' and we'd all start running, and everyone picked up a pomegranate and ran off with it and Mr Cox would come out raising his hand. You wonder how they made a living. You talk about children being naughty now – well, we were every bit as bad, but it was just devilment.

There used to be a cobbler down Church Street who had a bike and we didn't have bikes, but he agreed to let me ride his, so I'd take it up the North Road and come whizzing down again on this bike – but you couldn't do that now.

We used to have plays in the Methodist Church Hall and I'd be dressed up as a fairy or something. I went to the Parish Church – once in the morning, Sunday School in the afternoon and again in the evening. I know I used to fidget a lot.

When I was older we'd go up the Weston Hills with a bottle of lemonade and a sandwich. And a friend lived down Church Street and she'd sometimes say, 'Come on, me mum's out,' and we'd go to her house and she'd hack away at a loaf of bread and we'd have bread and condensed milk.

I used to love standing in the High Street and seeing the brewery carts with the sacks of malt. I can remember the smell of that malt, wasn't it lovely? You could smell it all round the town. The cart would stand in front of the brewery, under the hoist, and you could watch the sacks going right up the front and in at the top. That fascinated me. If I was late home from school, my mother would say, 'Have you been watching that brewery cart again?'

Children playing in Sun Street early 1920s.

A frolic of fairies prepare to meet their audience.

Just after the war, employment for the girls meant a choice between shop-work and going into service; boys and men could find a trade in brewing or farming, but the new Letchworth factories opened up more possibilities, and when the 'Bondor' came, it provided jobs for all.

Before I left school the local farmer used to come down to Pond Lane School about July time – that was Mr William Sale from Clothall. He'd come down to get volunteers to go in the harvest fields. The duty you got was to lead the horse and cart from shock to shock and then there was a man up on the cart and a man pitching the hay up to him, so your job was just to lead the horse. Yes I got 10/- a week for six weeks. That was a lot of money – mind you that was from about seven in the morning 'til seven at night and six days a week. We used to fall over each other to put our names down and he'd look us over and say, 'I'll have you, I'll have you, I'll have you,' and you was all fixed up with a job during the summer holidays. One year it was inclement weather and we had an extension for two weeks, so we had eight weeks' holiday instead of six- the authorities let us have the time off.

I began working at the Blacksmiths in 1915. Work started at 6.30 am and went on 'til 6.30 pm. Most of the work was shoeing horses as there was no motor transport in the early days. We also repaired agricultural implements, harrows, ploughs, rolls, etc. Horses were then practically the only means of transport; there were bakers' ponies, milk-cart ponies, brewery horse, butchers' vans' horses – even the midwife had a pony cart. We made all the shoes for the horses ourselves – now they're ready made.

In winter when frosts and snow prevailed, the horses all turned up for frost screws before they could start their journeys out to the different towns. As soon as winter started, shoes had to be made with snow holes ready to take the screws.

Mr F A Castle, blacksmith, photographed at his forge in the 1970s.

We made implements for the gas works – large iron coke barrows – all cut by hand with hammer and chisel – and 16 foot long rakes.

When we went to various factories to work, everything was done by hand, we had to take a ratchet, cramp and drill – it was very hard work.

All welding was done by forge-welding, oxygen welding hadn't begun then. In 1922, oxygen and gas cutting and welding came into being and Mr Roast, the blacksmith, was the first to install it in this district; it was a great help. One thing I did was to weld the eye of an ordinary sewing needle at Hatfield Show and this won a prize.

Mr Roast died in 1943 and then I carried on myself with extra help for the heavy work.

Times have changed – men used to walk to work or go on bicycles – no one had cars, they couldn't afford them. Now every Tom, Dick and Harry has one. I remember Mrs Goddard who lived in the corner house of the old cottages had a notice on her little gate. 'If you can read this, you're too damn near.' – that meant the motorist.

Accidents were the order of the day; when cars used to hit one another, out came the sheets and anything else available to tie up the dead and dying.

When I left school I started work at Moss's in Letchworth for 10/- for a 50-hour week – I was 14 then. I started as errand boy then at 15 I was apprenticed into the provision side – 8 to 6 weekdays, 8 to

Baldock Market re-opened in 1925 and for a few years it was principally for farmers to trade in sheep. People also recall going there to buy fish and hands of bananas for 6d.

7 Fridays, 8 to 8 Saturday, 8 to 1 half-day. For two or three weeks before Christmas we'd work anything up to 10 o'clock at night. I worked 'til 8 or 9 o'clock on Christmas Eve and the Christmas holiday was just two days. And we had lots of extra orders to prepare – hams, pork pies, sausages, crackers, special tins of biscuits, Christmas puddings – the shop did very well. We prepared quite a few whole hams, too, and packed them up in boxes for delivery. Most people managed to find a bit of money for a few extras at Christmas. Then, of course, there was the Christmas Club where people paid so much a week and had it put down on a card at the shop to save a bit for Christmas.

When the girls were leaving school, Miss Cutter used to ask, 'Does anyone want to go into service?' But no one did because by that time they could go and work at the Bondor, or in a shop, of course.

My Father was Fred Farr the baker and confectioner in Whitehorse Street, he was an expert in icing sugar. He used to make all sorts of cakes: he made macaroons whilst I made the doughnuts, the first one of the batch was always for me! He was a really good self-taught confectioner, his wedding cakes always used to be a year old. He'd soak them in rum, label them and put them up in the store cupboard, then decorate them as needed.

There was a lot of work attached to running a business in those days, you worked long hours. I can remember when I first got a job in London with the old LCC, I used to travel up by train every day.

Well, for three weeks before Christmas I used to come home off the train at a quarter-to-seven, have my dinner, go into the bakehouse, have another dinner at one o'clock, back in the

Many traditional craftsmen were still in business, including Bysouth, the wheelwright, in Park Street.

Farr's, the bakers, in Whitehorse Street, 1922.

bakehouse, go to bed at three, get up and catch the quarter-to-eight train, sleep on the train both ways and that's how it was. Hard work. At Christmastime a lot of people brought their dinners to be cooked in the bakehouse ovens, but not at other times, well, for one thing, father wouldn't work on a Sunday. He wouldn't start making the dough until twelve o'clock Sunday night, he was a very principled man.

By the mid-1920s my father was running the family bakery business in Whitehorse Street and a lovely old building it was, too, blending in with the rest of the street. In the 1970s the Council allowed it to be pulled down and replaced with the present mockery, which doesn't even have suitable windows to match the rest of the street.

At first we delivered the bread in a horse van and then with the motor van. With the brewery being so near, there were lots of rats about, so one of my jobs was to keep down the rat population; there was no reliable rat poison in those days, so they were more or less uncontrolled. However much we got rid of the rats from our premises, they'd come over from the brewery, and they were deadly. There was a rat-run right along the back of the High Street. I had a club, a torch and a jewel of a dog called Bill, a dedicated ratter. We'd bought him for £2 as a ratter, through the 'Exchange and Mart' and he was worth his weight in gold, rat-mad, he was! When we kept the horse, we had a manure heap at the top of the yard and every now and then I'd take a hose up and turn it on the heap to flush the rats out. I'd hold old Bill by his tail and when a rat came out I'd let go and if I didn't let go quick enough he spun round after my hand!

I used to have to go up the back, and one night I whipped up the bonnet of the van and there were four rats sitting on the cylinder block munching corn – we used to sell corn then – Bill got two on one side, I got one on the other, and the last one came up the inside of my trouser leg! I nearly went mad. I went down into the shop where Dad was working late and he had a bottle of whisky on the counter and he was most surprised when I dashed in and gulped some down!

Another time, there was a car parked across our entry, blocking us in. 'Shift it,' says Dad. So I reached my hand in to release the break and a terrier nearly took my hand off. 'You shift it,' I says, 'No, don't think I'll bother,' he says.

When I was at school we had a lot of fun tobogganing on Weston Hills and I had a very big sledge, most years someone got a leg broken or something sledging up there. In 1929 there was a really severe winter and all the lanes round about disappeared under snow. So my father fixed three tea-chests onto my sledge and with our old horse in front, we were able to deliver the bread to Wallington and Clothall.

I first went to work at Rabans, the builders in Sun Street, to do the book-keeping and general office work. I'd only been there a few days when I was asked to sew up some little white pillows filled with sawdust. What on earth could they be for I wondered? 'They're to go in the coffins, for the occupant's head to rest on' I was told! Of course, lots of builders were also undertakers in those days, but at 16 it wasn't something I liked to think about. However I soon got used to the sight of the coffin boards being bent into shape and the glue pot always bubbling away in the corner, although I was never very keen on seeing the finished article.

I had an indentured apprenticeship to the rag trade with Mr Jeffreys but I never finished it. They got all the papers, but I was so miserable there that I didn't carry on. We used to work from nine in the morning until seven at night every day and from nine in the morning until nine at night on Saturdays, all this for 5/- a week – and I was reduced to tears nearly every day.

It was very strange because this couple who ran the business were killed by rags. They were walking by Pattersons and a lorry came by loaded with rags, and the load came off just at that corner – she was killed outright and he lived a bit longer.

I stayed at school till I was 15, then I was apprenticed to Booths. Mr Abraham Booth and Mrs Booth came to our house and I said, 'Mum, Mrs Booth is at the door. I wonder what she wants.' And Mrs Booth said 'I hear your daughter, Phyllis, would like to work in a shop.' Ever since I was four years old I always wanted to work in a shop. I had to sign a contract for five years and I got 5/- a week. It got up to 25/- after five years.

Booths was a nice place to work, the money was poor but you did learn there – the apprentice system was very good. There were silks, cottons, hooks and eyes, and press studs and I had to learn the haberdashery drawers off by heart so you could go to the right drawer straight away. I had a very strict supervisor and I reckon she made me go over those drawers fifty times before she was satisfied I knew them. And woe betide me if she opened a drawer and there was a reel of cotton missing of the colour she wanted. I'd have to go upstairs to the store and get the right one and fill the drawer up again.

My first job was at Mr Patterson's hardware shop, for 5/- a week. I used to have to dust all the brand new pans and things and the new bicycles and then serve in the part of the shop where they sold soap and shoe leather and crockery and stuff like that. I was only 15 and they didn't like it if I called their son 'Jack'. I don't suppose Jack was much older than I was but I was told, 'You must call my son, Mr Jack!'

I started on 7/6d a week in the building trade in 1924 and later went to 12/6d. If it rained and you couldn't do any work, you didn't get paid, nor for holidays. The first paid holiday I had was after I came out of the army, but it was unheard of for anyone to go away for a holiday. The Bondor made the town by bringing work in.

I worked for Mr Raban the builder, and he went round to Cambridgeshire and Essex doing work. They did restoration work on the Cambridge Colleges.

I also joined the Fire Brigade as call boy. When the fire bell went I had to cycle round telling the men in case the wind was in the wrong direction and they hadn't heard the bell. Then later – the early 30's, I joined the Fire Brigade proper. Nearly all the fires we had to deal with were farm fires. We were called out one evening to a fire and spent the night driving round Ashwell and Newnham looking for it.

I went to school in Clothall. My first job was in 1930 with Percy Thompson, the photographer over Quenbys, from December to Easter. Then I was introduced to A W Patterson and I started with him for 10/- a week with the promise of a raise of 2/6d at the end of the month. I went on to do cycle repairs and was errand boy at the same time until the war when I went into the armed forces.

I came back to Pattersons and stayed for a total of 37 years until he closed. I used to be in Patterson's workshop and could see right up the High Street. I've seen locomotives and barges come through on trailers. We always knew when royalty was coming through as the policeman used to come down, don his white gloves and stop all the traffic.

Working conditions at Pattersons were quite good but there

Patent medicines were popular as they were cheaper than a visit to the doctor.

were always several people waiting on the Cross outside for my job and they would occasionally come in and say, 'I'll do his job and work for you cheaper than him.' We repaired the bicycles upstairs and if there was anyone we didn't like, we'd loosen the bolts on their saddles.

I came up from Sussex and I thought how smart the girls were who worked at the Bondor. My sister worked there. I came to work at South Lodge. I was in the kitchen. We were paid monthly. The first week you were rich but by the end of the month, you were broke and we had to pay our insurance stamp and sometimes we hadn't saved the money for it. We had a dance up there once and we worked rather late and were all given 10/-. The wages at the Bondor were good. When I went home to Sussex and told my family what they earned, they couldn't believe it.

I can remember the people coming from Mansfield and so on when the Bondor took over. They were foreigners to us – we couldn't understand them and they couldn't understand us, but after a while we all got on and some of them married Baldock people.

I worked at Kayser Bondor for 46 years. I started about a year after it opened – I got about 30/-. My sister was apprenticed in the rag trade and got 5/-. Kayser paid well.

The coming of the Bondor made the town and it gave employment at a time when agricultural jobs were going. Some people left Letchworth factories to go to work there, but of course, there was also a big influx of people from the north – Leicester, Mansfield and Nottingham – all the skilled workers came from there. They did make others a bit envious, because the Bondor workers were the highest paid around here. They had a different way of life, too. They were very houseproud and had the money to buy things, because they came from the hosiery trade which had always paid big money.

There was a Sports and Social Club there and they took the Sports Club money out of your wages every week. They had a tennis court and a cricket club. And I belonged to the League of Health and Beauty in the 30s. Then a swimming pool was built there before the war.

I thoroughly enjoyed working there and there was a good canteen. Then the John Goodenday Centre was built after the war. In those days the girls would bicycle in from all over – Biggleswade and Weston and Sandon in all weathers, but it was worth the effort for the money. There were all different jobs – seaming, mending, linking, examining.

I think the Bondor spoiled Baldock – the people earned four or

'The Bondor girls.'

five times more than the people in the town – agricultural labourers and the like – and they showed it and it caused resentment. I remember standing in Moss's for a couple of slices of ham when a woman from the Park, as we called it, came in and pushed in front of me and demanded a pound of ham and, of course, they fell over themselves to serve her. Bondor workers could buy new things and change their furniture round and they'd try to run things and tell the Baldock people what they could do. I remember one woman had made a fancy loaf and she brought it into church for harvest thanksgiving and it was up on the altar Saturday and Sunday, and on Sunday evening when they were clearing up and parcelling up what had got to go to the hospital she came in and said to me, 'Where's my loaf?' and I looked at her and she said, 'I've come for my loaf.' 'Oh,' I said, 'you only lent it to the Lord, then, you didn't give it?' *And* she took it.

And there was a fuss when the houses were built and they wanted to change the name from New Road to Mansfield Road. We had our own council then and Mr Deans, he kicked up a fuss about it and he didn't think it should be changed, but they talked him out of it. The men were down here in lodgings before the houses were built. It brought employment to the town for lots of young people, though, but the older ones resented it.

The Bondor was a very good thing indeed for the town. A lot of people got a living at the Bondor. They were well off in comparison to other people living here. It ran football and cricket teams and you could play tennis. It provided alternative employment to farming, brewing or service for the girls.

When we came to Baldock, the Bondor had just started and they were looking for people to put them up. We had three Germans who came to set the machinery up. We went to whist drives in the canteen at the Bondor.

We used to come in twos or threes every fortnight from Wales to work at the Bondor. I came from Ebbw Vale and the gas lights used to fascinate me. It was dark when we came out of work – just the faint glow from the gas lamps – not the bright electric light I'd been used to.

I always wrote home once a week when I first came here and my mother wrote back and said, 'I don't know what sort of place you've gotten into, but all you seem to mention is the pubs.' There were a lot of pubs – I never went in them, but I mentioned them to let her know what the place was like.

I stayed with Mrs Kefford when I first came to Baldock from Wales; there was no electric light so we went to bed by candlelight. We had a good time there – there were no restrictions – we had to be in by 10 o'clock but that wasn't too bad. I think she used to vet our boyfriends though – some got asked in more than others.

The folding and boxing department at Kayser Bondor. The stockings would be put in boxes and sent down to Wood Street, Cheapside, where they were distributed to various shops. Stockings were also sent on from there to America.

Girls in the mending department at the Bondor.

We were very careful what we did because Welsh lads had been a bit of trouble in Baldock – they were living in Letchworth but were not made welcome there.

After a while, only the ones who'd been to grammar school were sent to work at the Bondor from Wales because they only wanted their best to go.

The first job I had was sizing – checking to see if the stockings were the same size. Then I became a seamer. They used to give us a Christmas Party at the Icknield Hall in Letchworth. When I started, there were about 30 seamers, later there were 150.

I came to Baldock in 1931 to work at Kayser Bondor. Girls on piece work there could earn £5 or more a week, while the average wage of their fathers was £2 10s 0d.

It's often said that Baldock was a poor town, but I didn't think it was. Coming here from London, from a family of seven children, 'breakfast' didn't mean anything to me, neither did 'tea' come to that, we'd have bread and dripping or something like that – and I'd been at work 18 months before I came to Baldock. But I came here and, low and behold, the people that I lodged with worked at the Bondor and I used to get a cooked breakfast *every morning* and that had been unheard of back home. In London I had worked for Kayser Bondor, which was the selling side of the Full-Fashioned Hosiery Company, and when the war broke out they decided that the showroom and the warehouse should be moved to Baldock. It was already laid on that *if* war broke out we were all to report to Kings Cross Station if we wanted to move with it. I really think my life started when I came to Baldock, because my standard of living went up in leaps and bounds.

The Bondor still operated during the war – the knitting carried on – one or two departments went out to various places – one went to Morch's Garage at the bottom of Royston Road.

Cosmos moved into the Kayser Bondor from Brimsdown and they made cathode ray tubes. Some people came up from Enfield with them and others were employed from here. The biggest tube must have measured 18 inches across and they all had to be blown.

South Lodge, like Elmwood Manor, needed a considerable staff to cope with the cosmopolitan life led by its owners, Mr and Mrs Terence Eden. Mr Eden travelled to London regularly on business and a month or two would be spent fishing or grouse shooting in Scotland; but the family, and Mrs Eden in particular, took an active interest in Baldock, too.

I was born in Hitchin in 1913 and came to Baldock in 1928 to work at South Lodge for Mr Eden who eventually became Lord Auckland. I started as the 'odd boy' and finished up as his personal chauffeur. I had to chop wood and get all the coal in for the bedrooms and see that there were plenty of logs for the dining rooms. There were six guest bedrooms and nine for servants and all occupied – two nannies for the children. The Edens bought the house from Mr Balance.

We worked long hours particularly when I became a driver. I didn't sleep in until I was 18 and started to drive. Then I had to sleep on the premises, either here or in London or we used to go to Scotland a lot – there were two houses in Scotland. I used to travel with him wherever he went.

They used to entertain quite a lot especially at weekends with shooting parties at Wallington, Quickswood and Sandon – we used to go all round there, shooting in the fields. And I had to make sure they had plenty to eat and drink and take it to them, then bring it back. Then I'd have to meet them to bring them all home again. We used to have a big shooting brake in those days – it was an 18-seater, so it took all the guns and the visiting keepers and we employed beaters from the asylum and they got 1/- a day and their lunch, and every so often Mrs Eden would send me down to Allnuts to buy them all a packet of cigarettes.

Mr Eden was a stockbroker and he'd bring all his friends down from London, there was Lord Crawley and Lord Onslow, Wills the cigarette people, and Walker, the whisky people. He was an old

Etonian and had lots of shooting friends. Edens dealt at Moss's and Worbey's, then later Mrs Eden went to Cooper's as well and the International and Piper's and Fry's. She split her custom up between several of the businesses in the town so they all had a share after one or two complained they were being left out.

The Edens had a nanny and a nursemaid to look after the two boys and one day the nanny came back with some oranges she'd bought at the Co-op and Mrs Eden made her take them back because no way would she deal at the Co-op. I used to use the car at election times to pick people up for the voting. The favourite was Loss Pettingell, although he was a Labour man, she always let me go round for him. Mrs Eden supported all the candidates when they put up – Sir Arnold Wilson and Lord Lindgren were parliamentary candidates and Dr Riddell and Sid Grey, from The George and Dragon, were local candidates – oh yes, she used to take an active part in the life of the town – she was President of the Football Club, too.

We had a butler, two footmen, head housemaid, under housemaid, cook, assistant cook and scullery maid, two gardeners and a help; we had a dogman, too. Mrs Eden had six in her bedroom – spaniels, retrievers, setters and then they had six labradors in the kennels behind the old Anchor pub where the Catholic Church now is. One day Mrs Eden was walking to the kennels and she fell through the ground. When they found her, they discovered a tunnel from the old pub (which was now a private house) into the Weston Hills. Then they had it filled in.

I carried on with Mr Eden (or Lord Auckland as he was then) and joined the army with him. I stayed with him until his discharge in 1942. Then I rejoined the Regiment. After the war he came to see me every Sunday – he never missed a Sunday until the day he died.

After the war I worked for Mr Grey at The George and Dragon, then I worked at the brewery and finally went to work at the Kryn and Lahy until I retired. It was hard work there – such a change from working for the Edens, where the hours were sometimes long but the work wasn't hard. I never had a regular day off, though, because I always had to be there if I was needed. But sometimes he'd go off for the weekend and I wouldn't be required so then I got the weekend off. And they were such nice people to work for. She loved dancing, there were lots of dances in the Town Hall. Every now and then she'd say, 'I think we'll have a dance, William. Here's a couple of tickets for you and your girl. You go and pick up the piper from Stevenage.' She used to hire him from the Scots Guards in London – Pipe Major Robinson – he even made records after the war. She always had a dinner party beforehand and he'd get dressed up in all his uniform and go nearly to the top of Weston Hills where there was a long meadow and he'd play his pipes.

The High Street with the old Boot public house and South Lodge at the far end.

HIGH ST. BALDOCK

Then he'd come down and walk around the table still playing his pipes and the boss used to give him a glass of whisky and then they'd all go to the dance – and there'd be the Lancers and the Eightsome Reel and all dances like that. The staff all had their orders to ask Lady Auckland to dance with them.

There was a dance one night at the George and Dragon and about three in the morning she says, 'I think it's time we had breakfast,' so about half-past-four we all sat down to sausage and mash and champagne. They were lovely days.

Fêtes and bazaars continued to draw the crowds at weekends, and the cinema was an old favourite, but more people were turning to sport as a form of relaxation, particularly when the Bondor provided such excellent facilities.

We used to have Sunday School treats in the field on Weston Way where the fire station now is and I remember one year Mr and Mrs Blanks had a stall up there selling ripe red gooseberries and if we won a penny or ha'penny on the races then we'd aim for the gooseberries. This was the Methodist Sunday School – Dad was a lay preacher there – they used to call them local preachers then.

I remember the Flower Shows, they were lovely; they were run by Michael Sands and Johnny Booth, on August Monday, it was always a nice day. The Show was held where the caravan park is now, up Limekiln Lane. There used to be a big field at the top there and they were held in that. There were all the prizes for vegetables and flowers and flower arrangements and things like that. There was also a prize for the best collection of wild flowers and we came third with our wild flowers one year. I can remember the smell of the flowers in that marquee now, beautiful, and with all the girls in their summer dresses it was lovely. They also had a fancy dress competition – my sister and I went as Jack and Jill one year. Yes, it was always a fine day, August Bank Holiday Monday, it never rained.

Mr A H Cross conducting an augmented choir and orchestra in a performance of The Messiah in the Town Hall, 1927.

We always went in the procession, all dressed up; the first one I can remember going in, my mother dressed me up as an advertisement for Primrose Soap, which was a well-known make at that time. She sent off to the firm for things to put on the dress and

The Congregational Church,
Baldock.

Thursday, Nov. 24th, 1927.

**CHORAL
CENTENARY
CELEBRATIONS.**

Handel's Sacred Oratorio,

"The Messiah,"

will be rendered by the choir, augmented by friends from Letchworth, Royston and District, in the

BALDOCK TOWN HALL.

The following principals are expected.

Mrs. Kenneth Spinks,   Miss Ivy Powell,
(Soprano), Letchworth.   (Contralto), Royston.
Mr. C. S. White,   Mr. F. Godwin,
(Tenor), Stevenage.   (Bass), Letchworth.

THE EXCELSIOR ORCHESTRA.
(augmented)

Conductor : Mr. A. H. Cross.   Pianist : Miss Olive Cross.

Chorus and Orchestra of 60 Performers.

Doors open 6.45.   Commence 7.30.

ADMISSION   PROGRAMME.
Reserved Seats -   2/0 (including tax)

A nursery-rhyme group photographed at the back of St Mary's Church Hall, Whitehorse Street 1923.

Tea ladies at the Horticultural Show, August Bank Holiday 1925.

Children deciding how to spend their money at the side-shows.

Two fancy dress contestants take part in a Hospital Day fund-raising event.

back they came. I had a purple hat and little white socks and a poster of the soap to carry on a card. My sister went as a dolly in a box and she was carrying a little dolly in her hands, dressed just the same as she was. She won first prize and I got a 'Highly Commended', because they said you couldn't have two prize-winners in one family. But my mother sent a photograph of me up to the Primrose Soap people and we got the most gorgeous box of soaps back, as many different kinds of fancy soaps as you can imagine.

We used to go to the Sunday School treats in Morris's Meadow. Fish paste sandwiches, slab cake and bring your own mug. We used to think it was wonderful – it *was* wonderful!

Then we'd go to the Baldock Cinema in Whitehorse Street, not every week, but we liked to go. We'd say to my father, 'Dad, give us tuppence, we want to go and see Pearl White, she was nearly killed last week and we want to see if she's all right.' You see they'd run these serials, which always ended with her tied to a railway line, or dangling over a cliff or something like that. Then he'd say, 'Right, I've got a funeral on this afternoon, you get out my top hat and go over it with the velvet duster, and you nip out to Newlings and get me a new collar.' So we dashed round and got our tuppences as he went out.

I'd got younger brothers and sisters and it was always my job to look after them and we used to like to go to the cinema on a Saturday afternoon about 5 o'clock. And one week Mother told me to take the youngest one along with us. And I didn't want to, I said, 'She'll only cry.' but Mother insisted. So off we went the three of us, and we got in and the big lights went out, then the side lights went out and as soon as the lights went out she started to cry and wouldn't stop so we had to come out. The same thing happened the next week, so when we got outside, I slapped her and Mrs Serocold happened to be going by. 'Oh, you are an unkind girl,' she said. 'Well,' I said, 'nobody's going to spoil your entertainment, but she's just spoiled mine.' When I got home and told Mother she didn't tell me off, she just said, 'Whatever made you answer her like that?' 'Well,' I said '. . . I was *cross!*'

We used to have lovely flower shows and fetes up at the back of South Lodge when the Bishells kept it. She was a real country lady with the tweed suit and pearls, big lady really but very nice. They had fancy dress and a fete and in the summer time there was one in the street here, not on the scale it's done now, but the town was smaller then. I remember going to the fete one year, just after I was married, and there was a boxing booth there in the evening and we got there late and had to stand at the back behind some men in bowler hats, and I got a bit carried away and brought my fist down onto one of the bowlers. My husband caught hold of my arm and snatched me off and said, 'You're not coming with me again!'

Baldock Cinema and cinema café, Whitehorse Street.

We went to Wicksteed Park with the Sunday School when it first opened. The Wesleyan Guild held a social evening once a week with speakers sometimes. And we put on a play once called 'Princess Juju.'

There were the Sunday School outings, by train to Hunstanton. The train took you practically onto the beach, so it was out of the train with your bucket and spade and straight onto the beach.

I remember going to a picnic in a Mr Inskip's field at Shefford or somewhere, there was always a scramble for boiled sweets. He'd get them out of a big jar and throw them up in the air – but I never did get one! It was always the boys who got them, and they were hard – like coloured stones.

I remember Len Moore, now, he used to have outings for the children, I was ever so small then and never went but he always

Church outing to Yarmouth, early 1920s.

Eggs were collected and distributed to local hospitals at special 'Egg Services'.

put on a Christmas Party in the Town Hall for all the Baldock children. You used to go and say poetry and have competitions and things like that. And the children were taken on outings in open-top charabancs. It was tragic, because he died quite young, he fell out of a horse and cart on the Royston Road and was killed. Very sad, that.

We didn't have many outings but I do remember going to the British Empire Exhibition in Olympia in 1926 I think it was. We went in a charabanc – it wasn't a bus – and it was called The Optimist. There was another one called The Bluebell. Len Moore was very famous for arranging outings for the children to the sea and they would go in The Bluebell or The Optimist.

The first time I saw the sea I was 19. I served my apprenticeship at the Laker. I played for Cyril Bishop's football team and he asked me if I'd like to go to scout camp and I says, 'How are you going?' And he says, 'By bike.' Well I didn't have a bike but I told me mum and she borrowed a bike from Cannons the chemist where she used to do a bit of charring and a bit of washing. We went in 1921 and so I went on the bike – after a couple of spills. We camped at a village – Saxmunden – beautiful holiday it was. We went for a fortnight and we never had a spot of rain.

The Stanley Bishop Zoo at Jaywick Sands was quite well-known. Every summer he had this zoo with parrots and monkeys and the odd snake and so on and then in the winter he'd bring them all to Baldock and put them in the cellar, I should think, or kept them out at the back. They were both characters, well you had to be in that sort of line. For a time they even had a mermaid at the Zoo!

In the early 30s, Teddy Cooper, a local butcher, used to kill an ox and trail it around Baldock on one of Shelvoke and Drury's solid-tyred trailers. I think the proceeds of the collection went to Letchworth Hospital. He then used to put it up in Park Estate

Len Moore with the 'The Bluebell' about to set off for Clacton, August 1926.

Cyril Bishop (seated, centre, on grass) and scouts, 1922.

Stanley Bishop's zoo at Jaywick Sands.

near what is now Tesco's and the local unemployed turned the spit and roasted the ox. Then it used to be carved up and auctioned. It was quite a skilled job roasting the ox and the sweat used to pour off the men turning the spit.

Over 50 years ago cricket and hockey were played at the back of the old Kayser Bondor factory with tennis, bowls and swimming at the front. Fencing, table tennis and chess were some of the indoor activities.

Old Heath Hall had a very popular tennis court and club there. Netball was very keenly supported by various ladies teams, often entering teams in Letchworth interworks competitions. Boxing matches were held in the Baldock Town Hall around 50 years ago. These were organised by Letchworth Ascot Boxing Club, some of the Baldock members later joined the Bondor club. Badminton grew very popular after the Second World War and now continues at the old Town Hall.

During the Second World War, table tennis was provided at St Mary's Church Hall by the St Christopher's Group for the refugees, soldiers and members. Darts was also included. Baldock Social Club also provided snooker and billiards.

Pond Lane and St Mary's School pupils held all their field sports in the field on which Knight Templar School now stands, this previously being partially orchards. The Civil Defence practised their field activities there during the Second World War.

I really enjoyed working at the Bondor. There was a Sports Club and Miss Smith taught us how to play hockey and we moved on to play for Letchworth Ladies. She also taught us to play tennis. We played at St Christopher's Group because Mrs Prideaux had a court in her garden.

We used to go dancing in Icknield Halls and come home down the cinder path in our stockinged feet because our feet hurt with all the dancing – five or six of us young men and women.

Many years ago a Junior Imperial League was started – now the Young Conservatives, and when Mrs Eden came to live at South Lodge before the Second World War, she used to have dances up

The High Street 1940.

there and we used to go up there to lots of things and I remember dancing with Lord Knebworth – he was the MP and I remember Sir Arnold Wilson. He gave blood for a transfusion for Loss Pettingell and he was strong Labour and the joke was, would he now turn Conservative with Conservative blood in him!

Baldock was not in the front line during the Second World War, but everyone felt its impact. Women without school-age children were put on war-work, men who were not eligible for the forces joined the Home Guard or the ARP, families had to adjust to having evacuees living with them, and everyone had to cope with rationing.

It must have been at the time of the Munich crisis, 1938, when the army descended on our farm. They just arrived and took over half of it, even our house – the stairs went up the middle and we had one side and the army had the other! Officers slept in the house and they laid on electricity from a generator for their half whilst we still had oil lamps in our part, but since they didn't like going up the stairs in the dark, they lit that as well, and it was quite a novelty to push a little switch at the bottom of our stairs and see the light come on.

They used a big empty chicken hut as a canteen and they had a searchlight in the meadow and to me there seemed to be soldiers

Territorial volunteers, Ray Wilsher and Hugh Gilby, photographed on 2 September 1939.

Clara Carrot

The spice of life is very much Clara Carrot's concern; for she's a master of variety — a quick - change artist with a hundred and one disguises, each more amusing than the last. If you've only met her plain and boiled you've no idea how delightful she can be in other modes. You should try

Jugged Brisket

1½ lbs. brisket, 2 lbs. carrots, 2 tablespoons dripping, 1½ pts. vegetable stock, 1 tablespoon gravy thickening, 2 tablespoons piquant sauce or vinegar from pickle bottle, 1 saltspoon mustard. Melt the dripping in a stout saucepan. Grate half the carrot into it. Put in the meat, then the rest of the grated carrot. Pour in 1 pint stock. Cover saucepan, simmer 2 hrs. Thicken rest of stock with gravy thickening. Add sauce and mustard, pour into pot and cook fast for 10 mins. A grand dish, to serve 4 or 5.

everywhere, with my father farming round them so to speak. But when Chamberlain came back from Munich with his 'Peace in our time', they pulled out and went away.

When the Midlands were being raided, we'd often hear German aeroplanes flying over and they'd sometimes dump their last bombs on us as they flew back to Germany. I remember one moonlit night we heard a lot of planes going over, and as they went they were dumping incendiary bombs which were starting fires all over the fields. However the important thing was that they missed both the farms and the stacks of hay and corn (it was about harvest time). As I came out of the back door I could see my father jumping up and down in the yard, shaking his fists at the sky and shouting 'Yah! Missed us you blighters, missed us!'

I think it was the next morning that old Charlie came along on his bike, he'd been over the fields where Clothall Common houses now are, picking up unexploded incendiary bombs and he'd got them all on the carrier of his bike! My father certainly didn't want them and sent him off to take them along to the Police Station.

Then the war came and the blackout and you were called up either to go into the forces or into industry. And we had evacuees come. I remember them arriving and being trailed up the road in twos and my dad was so upset to see all these children that he dashed out and fetched two and we had two little sisters – they were lovely children from Tottenham.

The rationing was terrible. I gave up sugar for the children and I haven't taken it in tea since then. There were queues everywhere. Every shop you went into you had to queue.

Rationing made life difficult. I remember one greengrocer having some bananas in once and I queued up for them for quite a time and I got to the front and produced my child's ration book and said, 'I'd like some bananas, please.' 'Just a minute,' he said, 'You're not one of my regulars.' 'But I've got a child's ration book,' I said. But he wouldn't budge. 'I can't help that, these bananas are only for my regular customers.' But when I threatened to go to the Welfare Office, he called me back and said, 'Oh, all right, just this once then.'

During the war people would come round and spray factories and offices to get rid of germs, so that people wouldn't have to be away from work. Remember the slogan, 'Coughs and sneezes spread diseases'? There were other slogans too – 'Left on switches and turned on taps make happy Huns and cheerful Japs'!, 'Be like Dad, keep Mum' and 'Careless Talk Costs Lives'. In the paper they used to have 'Food Facts' issued by the Ministry of Food about using more potatoes to save ships. My Mother kept these and I've still got a recipe for chocolate cake using mashed potato. And we had to use dried eggs and dried milk, too.

There was Mr Strickland, the Food Officer who sat in the Council Offices and wielded a lot of power. He decided what allowances people could have: say extra cheese rations for farm workers, or if you had to eat sandwiches for your mid-day meal, or if you were a vegetarian, then you were entitled to extra cheese. Then expectant mothers got extra rations, bee-keepers got sugar for their bees at certain times of the year and Jews got extra sugar at Passover.

Rationing seemed to have had a gradual effect on what we ate, because things didn't become in short supply or difficult to get all at once, it was a gradual thing. Of course, if there were several of you in the family you were all better off, because, of course, you could pool your rations and work things out better to suit all of you. Our mother was very good at making a tasty meal and we had the vegetables out of the garden so we didn't do too badly. The only thing she wouldn't do was make pastry, as she'd been used to making very good pastry and you just couldn't make very good

Plan Your Savings for
BALDOCK, ASHWELL & DISTRICT'S
WARSHIP WEEK
MARCH 7th — 14th, 1942

Our Objective is £62,000
for H.M.S. "KIRKELLA" **(Trawler-Minesweeper)**

Baldock adopted trawler-minesweeper, HMS Kirkella, and raised funds for it through house-to-house collections during Warship Week.

pastry with the sort of ingredients you got during the war. So I got that job, as I didn't notice any difference! In fact the two years immediately after the end of the war were worse, you really did feel hungry then, because the rations were smaller and some things, like bread, were rationed for the first time.

There were 'Warship Weeks' and 'Tank Weeks' and 'Wings for Victory'. I can remember the parades marching down the High Street and turning right into Whitehorse Street, but I don't know where they went after that. There were the scrap metal drives and salvage and waste paper collections and, of course, we all had to 'Dig for Victory'.

Avenue Field was made into allotments and I'd help my aunt with hers during the war. I was still in St Christopher's Group. We helped the refugees.

Baldock was a pretty place then. The evacuees who came to Baldock didn't want to go back home. Although their first reaction was, 'What a god forsaken place – I'm not staying here long.' My dad said to one of them when they came in September, 'I'll take you blackberrying in October,' and he says, 'Oh, I won't be here that long.' But he was – we couldn't get rid of them in the end, they liked it so much.

Soldiers and 'tea ladies' in front of a wartime canteen set up in The Wilderness for all servicemen stationed in the town.

Baldock Secondary Modern School (now Knights Templar) had only just opened and almost straight away they had to share it with two evacuated schools. The Baldock children went in the morning and the Tottenham and Eastbourne children in the afternoon, and the church rooms in Whitehorse Street were opened up as schoolrooms for the extra junior-age children.

The children arrived by train and we met them at the station and took them to the Council Offices, I think, where they had cars to take them to wherever they were to go. I can see them now, the little ones with their gas masks round their necks and carrying little cardboard suitcases, they must have been terrified.

Some of the children trickled back, especially during the period of the 'Phoney War' as it was called, when nothing much seemed to be happening. But then of course, the raids started and unfortunately some of those families were killed. And some of them absolutely *hated* the country, it was so quiet and nothing much going on, they missed London's bustle and there wasn't much bustle about Baldock at that time, that's for sure!

The parents, or mothers rather, used to come visiting as often as they could, but it must have been hard for them. I don't think people realise what a wrench it must have been to send these little scraps away from home.

There was a youth club in Baldock Secondary Modern School run by the Headmaster, Mr Hancock. He'd been waiting for the school to be built for many years and it was opened in 1939. So

Members of the Army Cadet Force and their band c. 1944.

there he was, headmaster of this lovely new school, when war was declared, and immediately he had to share it with two other schools that had been evacuated here from Eastbourne and Tottenham. He started the Youth Club more or less straight away in 1940. There were musical evenings, either playing records or he'd get a pianist down. There was table tennis, the Girls Training Corps met there and so did the Army Cadets. There were dances and sewing classes, painting and cookery.

It's difficult to describe the atmosphere at the youth club, there was something going on all over the school. Baldock then was a hive of activity. There was no loutish behaviour and there were very few people who didn't take advantage of the facilities there.

We had soldiers here all through the war, Baldock was a garrison town. The army took over all the big houses. There were the Royal Engineers in The Wilderness and I think the Royal Artillery were in the Brewery House and they were in Cambridge House too, I think. They used them as billets. There were also the King's Own Yorkshire Light Infantry, but I think most were out in one of the villages, but some were billeted in the town. They manned a searchlight up at Bygrave. Letchworth Gate was closed all through the war, that's where they had the tank repair shops, they'd be Royal Engineers, I suppose, and there were the Tank Corps here too, of course. There were lines of tanks up there and repair pits and so on.

There was never any trouble as far as I can remember, everyone got along very well – I think the trouble came later when our allies arrived! The Americans were stationed out of the town, Bassingbourn and Litlington and the fighter base at Guilden Morden. You've heard of the 'Passion Wagon' – that came into the town to pick the girls up? They were chaperoned at first, but I'm not sure about later on . . . Of course, you've got to remember that our boys were in their big old boots and rough khaki uniforms whilst the GI's wore *shoes* and *ties* and had a much smarter uniform. They were much better paid too, and then, being brought up on Hollywood films, a lot of the girls thought that all Americans lived on ranches and owned acres of land! On the whole, the Americans were very polite and very well-spoken, very respectable.

There was no entertainment as such laid on for the troops in the town, but perhaps *they* didn't need it so much as those stationed in camps miles from anywhere. We used to play netball against them, us girls against a team of men; then they'd move on and we'd play against the next lot. Then after the match there'd be baked beans on toast in The Fourteenth Century Tea Rooms – that was their 'entertainment', poor chaps! Still, being away from home, they probably appreciated the friendly atmosphere.

Troops were stationed all over the town and endless convoys passed through. We rushed out when the American convoys came in as they always threw chocolate and chewing gum to us – they were very generous. We were only allowed 2ozs of sweets a week so we sucked Victory V's, Rennies and Little Imps instead!

Many planes crashed in the area and we hurtled off on our bikes to see the wreckage. I remember seeing the American Flying Fortresses going over in close formation when suddenly the wings of two of them touched, the planes broke up and pieces floated

US servicemen and local girls enjoy a day out on the Weston Hills, 1943.

| PURFLEET 6.9.40. 1 | PURFLEET 8.9.40. 2 | PURFLEET 9.9.40. 3 | PURFLEET 10.9.40. 4 | SOUTHAMPTON 2.12.40. | LEICESTER 23.12.40. | LONDON 19.3.41. | NORWICH 8.4.40. | NORTHAMPTON 11.4.41. | LONDON 17.4.41. |

1939 - Baldock - 1945

KINGSLEY. DELLAR. LILLEY. WESTWOOD. ARMISHAW. TRIGG. SCRIVEN. HART. PATEMAN. WILLIAMS. MAYES. COX.
LEETE. GALE. FARR. RIDLEY. TANSLEY. MALES. SMITH. BY-SOUTH. SWAIN. WARNER. GENTLE. CROSS. DEANS. BYGRAVE.
GRAVESTOCK. TURNER. BARKER. EDMONDS. CRIMSTON. ARBURY. BROWN. PAYNE. LEE. BY-SOUTH. CARMER. YOUNG. LEE.
CASTLE   ALBONE   SKINNER   WALKER   KEECH

LOCAL FIRES 166

ANYWHERE ANYTIME

LOCAL REINF. 80

down behind the Weston Hills. There were 20 men in those two planes. Aircraft wreckage would sometimes be brought through the town on lorries which pulled up at a café here and stayed overnight. We saw our chance and climbed up into the broken fuselage and played pilots while no-one was looking!

I went in the army in late 1941 but before that I was in the Fire Brigade. I was on a roaming team – we used to be called out if there was any bombing – we'd down tools and go where there was a fire. I went to London and Shellhaven, Peacehaven and Bath.

I saw the blitz in London all round the Guildhall and I remember seeing one building on fire next to a big hospital and Phil Lee and me had to go up onto the top of the building to damp down surrounding buildings.

We used to go all over the South Midlands region entering competitions with the Fire Brigade.

I was in the Home Guard and as we didn't get much rifle practice I often thought if the time ever came when we had to use our rifles we'd probably injure as many of our own as the enemy! We once went on night manoeuvres and were given a bit of a feed at the Knights Templar School. One chap complained of stomach

As well as fighting fires in London, Baldock Fire Brigade also travelled as far afield as Norwich, Southampton and Leicester during the war.

ache afterwards – I put it down to the dumplings – they were hard, no doubt about it!

One platoon of the Home Guard met in the Black Eagle, but there were several different platoons around the town. This one had Sergeant Endersby and Sergeant Astor in charge.

The pill-boxes were at all the road junctions, then there were the ARP posts like the one at the end of Football Close, and we'd often walk into the tank traps in the dark. These really came too late when the main threat was over. At the height of it all, we had no uniforms, just armbands and I think there was just one rifle and 10 rounds of ammunition in Baldock. It really was pikes and rakes and things. A lot of villages had nothing and we trained with broom sticks at first, so it wasn't until the threat had really died down that we got kitted out with uniforms. One of our jobs then was guarding the water works on the Willian Road, there were six of us and we'd do one hour on and two hours off, during the night. We had a rifle and a round of five bullets and when you changed over, you'd take them out of your pocket and pass them on to the next man on guard duty – you never had them in the rifle. If a parachutist came down in the dark, what we were to do I just don't know. If anyone came through the gates you'd have to say, 'Who goes there, stand and be recognised . . .' But you still hadn't got anything in your rifle. You weren't allowed to do that unless you had orders from the sergeant in charge.

I was with the 'Wotsanames' when we went to entertain the troops at the anti-aircraft battery up by Biggleswade water tower. It was about the time of Dunkirk or soon after and just as we were leaving, after putting on the show, the commanding officer came up to me and said, 'Look,' showing me his service revolver, 'I don't suppose you happen to know where I might get some bullets for this, do you? I really would like to be able to load it, you know, just in case . . .' Well, I recommended a hardware and gunsmiths shop in Hitchin and gave him the address. I happened to see him in the town a couple of weeks later. 'Thank you so much,' he beamed happily, 'they let me have six!'

There were Italian prisoners-of-war at the maltings on the Royston Road. They kept them there and they mostly worked on the land round about. Then German POW's were kept in the huts up London Road near where the flats are now in Chiltern Road. After the war the camp was used to house Polish refugees unable to return home.

Everybody 'fire-watched' everywhere. I fire-watched in the Church, on the Council Offices, on the school and at work, in Letchworth – and Letchworth on a Sunday afternoon. . . . Oh dear. . . .

If you were lucky you spent most of your time either sitting or

A member of the 'signals corps' and despatch rider with the Home Guard.

Sergeant Endersby with his Home Guard platoon which met in The Black Eagle.

Vera O'Brien (second row, third from left) and her party of ladies, knitting for servicemen.

lying down asleep, but, of course, if there was an alert you had to get up and look as if you knew what you were doing! There was supposed to be one man to two girls – men being in short supply – but if there was an alarm, as like as not the man would say, 'Well I'm off, I'm supposed to be the ARP warden over at so and so.' Many was the time that my friend and I were left like that – the whole of Baldock Secondary Modern School in charge of two sixteen-year-old girls!

Fortunately, we never had to do anything, but from the top of the church you could see all sorts of lights if there were air-raids on. You could see the glow in the sky if London was being bombed and flashes too, and, of course, the searchlights could be seen from miles away.

Junior members of Vera O'Brien's concert parties.

I don't know what we would have done in an emergency, I seem to remember that at the Secondary Modern School the stirrup pump was up on the roof, which is where they thought it would be needed, but to get to it you had to climb up a rope ladder in the dark. That would have been interesting . . .

I think the only attack on the town was when some enterprising character flew along the railway-line and machine-gunned the station; perhaps he'd had a disappointing day, anyway he shot up the station, but nobody was hurt.

The air-raid sirens often went, but after the first few times people didn't take too much notice. For one thing, you often knew there was an air-raid before it went off, because we could always hear the hum of the machinery from the Kryn and Lahy – that big foundry works which used to be in Works Road, Letchworth. You could hear the hum of that coming across the fields, and then if you were walking back from the cinema or somewhere at night and it suddenly went quiet, you thought 'Hello', they've shut off the Kryn,' because factories like that got advance warnings.

We had surface shelters here-and-there around Baldock, brick walls with flat concrete roofs, and the Council came round and built 'blast walls' outside the window of whichever rooms in the house they decided were the safest. In our case it was the kitchen, and they built this wall about eight feet high and some 18 inches away from the window.

Then some people had indoor 'Morrison' shelters, made of steel and wire mesh, and others had the 'Anderson' shelters in their gardens; they were made of corrugated iron, partly sunk in the ground and covered with earth. I know one of our neighbours built a rockery over theirs; it's still there as far as I know. People who lived in the shops usually went down into their cellars, I believe.

I used to go to Miss Rose's hairdressers shop, I'd have a 'Eugene Perm' for 21s 0d. There was this awful machine that you sat under and if there had ever been an air-raid alert, you'd have never got out because you were attached to it by all these wires. They used to come round with smelling salts in case you felt faint because it was so hot. Sometimes you'd smell burning, but you couldn't tell which wire it was that was burning your hair.

I planned on getting married at the end of the war because I thought, 'Well things are at their worst now, so it will be down hill from now on.' Instead of that, things got a great deal worse! After I was married we got half-a-pint of milk every other day and you didn't get fresh eggs sometimes for weeks on end. You were better off if you kept chickens and quite a few people did. Some kept a pig at the end of the garden, but you had to give half of it to the Government. You had the pleasure of rearing it and then you had half and they took the other half – well, I suppose they had to pay for it.

I can't remember much in the way of celebrations for the end of the war. I think people saved that up for when the boys came home, like the boys who'd been prisoners-of-war. Everybody put up 'Welcome Home' decorations when they thought the train was coming in with them coming home. But I can't remember parties, to be honest. I don't think there was very much to have a party with, everybody was pretty well worn out and then they were so glad it was all over. They saved their celebrations for when the boys came home and then people helped each other out with things to make it a real welcome. Of course some of the boys were such a long time coming home – those that had been out in the Far East, and been prisoners-of-war.

But there were lots of happy memories of the war, it was an awful time, but people did work together and there was a spirit of friendship, somehow, everybody was willing to help out.

Many Baldock men served overseas including Bill Beechener, photographed here in the Far East.

Light entertainment always provided a few hours' relief from the daily grind, and Mrs O'Brien and her amateur concert party 'The Wotsanames' found themselves in increasing demand.

My mother (Vera O'Brien) was born in New Zealand in about 1895 and she came to this country as a small girl when she was about 11 or 12. She was taught to dance by a Russian lady who soon

Vera O'Brien's Christmas pantomime in the Town Hall.

realised she was a natural dancer. Her grandmother was a brillant pianist who would play the piano for Mother and her sister to dance to. By the time she was 14, Mother was lead dancer in a touring pantomime going to places like Merthyr Tydfil and Northern and Southern Ireland.

When Mother started the shows with Mrs Waters, she was horrified because the attitude had always been that you only took your profits and Mother didn't agree with this. She said, 'If you do something for charity then you give everything to charity – scrounge someone who will print the programmes – you'll do everything, but every penny goes to charity.' You could almost work that out by the numbers of seats and what you charged for the seats. Everything had to be up front before the show started.

Mrs Waters said she wanted to do a pantomime if Mother would teach the dancing, which she did – that was Cinderella – the very first, and then a lady who lived in Hitchin Street did the dressing – it might have been old Mrs Hoeg. Mother decided she'd do her own thing the following year and she started to write all the shows because she had to pay £150 in royalties for the first one and Mother said, 'I'm not going to give £150 away for royalties, I'll write my own!' And what she did was, she went out and bought four or five different copies of the same pantomime by different people – you can buy them in London – and she pinched bits out of each one. And then everyone would help and change it from then on as they went along.

In 1939 a man arrived at the front door and wanted to see Mother. He said, 'I understand you do shows.' That was just after we'd finished doing 'Babes in the Wood', and he said, 'War has started and we know that there will be a lot of troops billeted in Hertfordshire in very small units, running searchlights and anti-aircraft guns. ENSA does not go to units under 250 men, and we're worried about the entertaining of them. We want to organise it so that the amateur people in Hertfordshire will do shows for them – would you be prepared?' So Mother said, 'Oh, yes – we can do a concert – there'll be no problem there.' So we said, 'Well, how do we get around?' He said, 'Well, that's easy – we'll arrange all transport. All you have to do is to be ready to be picked up at a fixed time and we'll deliver you where you want to go.' And that's what happened, and as far as I know we were one of the few who did it. We didn't come across many other shows. Often we didn't get home until one or two in the morning and we used to have to get up for work in a few hours' time.

Mother's theory was that the best thing to do for concert parties was to have a lot of pretty young girls and put as few clothes on them as decency would allow. That would always go down well with the troops.

When I think back to Mrs O'Brien, how she had us all in that

'Wotsanames' chorus line.

'Village girls' and friend taking part in the annual pantomime.

The war ended at last and Baldock's ARP stood down.

Manor House – the door was always open for us – night after night. Doris and I used to live down there and if we weren't rehearsing we'd go in the stables – the old coach house. They called it that 'cos that's where the coach was kept, as against the stables where the horses were kept. That became the Baldock Rhythm Club later on. She was a really lovely person.

When Mrs O'Brien started the 'Wotsanames' we used to go out about twice a week after work. We used to rehearse on Sundays. We had a discussion about the name we should call ourselves and I said we should call ourselves the 'Wotsanames' because nobody can ever remember the name of anybody, and it just stuck. The show 'Grin and Tonic' was in 1941. That replaced the pantomime more or less.

The whole of Baldock was involved then – I think most people had been in the shows or somebody in their family had. We never had any problems selling tickets – we'd run for a week and then have to run another week because it was so popular.

Mrs O'Brien had a very good sense of humour. She did a Charlie Chaplin routine in 1915. She was entertaining a whole lot of troops in the hospital. And one of them had had an operation and he had to be taken back to the theatre because he burst his stiches because he was laughing so much. Mother was absolutely horrified at this and she went to see how he was doing the next day and all he said was, 'It was worth it!'

The 'Wotsanames' started in 1940. I often wonder how many shows we did in all. We did one and sometimes two shows a week. We finished about 1944/45.

Mrs O'Brien received no recognition from the County for arranging so many concerts throughout the war.

Apart from organising shows, Mrs O'Brien also used to put up lots of soldiers for the night. She'd have them sleeping in the billiard room of the Manor House. There was usually somebody there and the police had a key and they were always dropping them in.

Post War
and Beyond
1945 to 1970

The war had been a great strain for everyone, particularly those with relatives and friends in the forces overseas. Now it was over and things would get better again. . . wouldn't they?

Life after the war was very drab and grey – everyone was worn out and I think it gradually dawned on us that we'd won the war but where had it got us? This drabness went on into the early 1950s. Many things were still rationed for years after. Mind you, I suppose, taking the population as a whole, a lot of them were better fed than they'd ever been before because if something was on ration they were jolly well going to have it. Children particularly, in some areas would have cod liver oil and orange juice that they hadn't had before.

The award-winning production of 'Children in Uniform'.

But there were bright sparks amid the gloom and Kate Behrens Steinfeld was one. A founder member of the Baldock Players, she tackled such classics as 'A Midsummer Night's Dream' and 'A Streetcar Named Desire'. A friend said of her, 'she just got the best out of you. . . she lived and breathed drama.'

'The Baldock Players' was founded in 1944 for the furtherance of adult education in drama and dramatic art, and Mr Hancock was the chairman. The first thing to be put on was four one-act plays. Kate Behrens Steinfeld came to Baldock early in the war and helped out with the St Christopher's Group – that's how we got interested.

We started with one-act plays that were put on in the Senior School, now Knights Templar, and the programme cost 3d. One programme has got Kate Steinfeld and Molly Booth on it. We took part in the British Drama League Festival. This was a big thing, the most exciting time we'd ever had. We put on a play in the Welwyn Festival and we were absolutely slated, they didn't

Road widening of Weston Way in the fifties when it still looked like a country lane.

like it at all. But one team dropped out, so they asked Mrs Steinfeld if she could put another one in. She had had the play 'Children in Uniform' translated from the German, and we put an excerpt from it in the Drama Festival – and they loved it! We were runners-up for the whole Festival. It was very exciting because, when we all filed in, there were all these girls in uniform and they stood up and clapped and that was lovely. Effie was marvellous – she was the young girl, Manuela. We were also in the daily paper – Nora Alexander was the columnist – The News Chronicle. She was so interested in us as young players that she came with us when we went to the Festival on the coach.

She did have a marvellous personality, Mrs Steinfeld, she was a real worker, she got the best out of people, she was wonderful. We did it for a week somewhere because we were asked to go. It was quite exciting.

Life in general, though, didn't get any easier. Rationing was still imposed and just when people thought things couldn't get any worse, winter came with a vengeance.

The winter of 1947 was sheer unmitigated hell – but colder! For 36 hours it snowed, with high winds and very low temperatures so you had drifting. It froze, of course, and when it stopped, the world had changed. I used to walk to work along the cinder path which went along the back of St Joseph's Convent from the top of West Avenue. There was this very high hedge that went all around and another one that went to the other side, along the field between the cinder path and the old highway and the railway line and you could come out at the end of Works Road as you do now. But during that winter we were walking on *top* of the hedge, because the snow was frozen solid and it was like that for weeks, long after the daffodils should have been out. And, of course, when it did eventually melt, I can remember that the field that's now Knights Templar sports field was like a sea, and it all came pouring through the gate and across the corner. And the first time I tried to cycle to work again – I went up Letchworth Road because I knew I wouldn't get along the cinder path – the water was flowing across the road and it came above the pedals, it was incredible, really.

The cinder path was very busy in those days and at one time there were more people coming down it to work in Baldock at the Bondor than going the other way. It was quite a long walk into the middle of Letchworth and we'd sometimes have lunch at the Carlotta Café in Leys Avenue and the only vegetable they'd got was swede, that's all there was, there were no green vegetables at all that winter and, of course, no frozen food; there was the odd tin of peas but not many of those.

We offered to carve our initals on the swede and have it back each day. Of course, the weather was so bad there was no fish to supplement the meat ration. And we lived in a cottage with outside plumbing, and for about three months, I think, we had to carry buckets across the next door neighbour's garden to the outside privy. We had terrible power cuts – coal was short and nothing was moving on the railways. It really was truly dreadful, because rations already were about as bad as they could be, but this very cold weather made it worse. It was April before things improved.

We could get coke for the fire at home from the gas works, but that was rationed. Then we got short of kindling wood so my husband cut a corner out of a bench that my father had made for him. And father was a great one for coming round and prowling in our cellar, I think it was a novelty as he hadn't got one, and he came round once and went down there after this chunk had been cut out of the bench. There was silence and he came back up the stairs and just looked at us and walked straight out of the front door! We'd roll newspapers up and light those but they didn't really work very well because they were so thin. And we'd make brickettes out of coal dust and cement.

There's a Rhona Roy dress for every occasion

The marriage of Princess Elizabeth and Prince Philip was a welcome diversion in November of that year, and the coronation six years later gave everyone an excuse to celebrate. A full programme of events was organised for the town and local street parties were held, too.

Well done, Baldock! was the unanimous verdict of everyone at the closing of the Baldock Coronation Festivities.

What a week it was! A tea-party for 184 elderly people, presentation of souvenirs to over 1,000 schoolchildren, street tea parties for the children, competitions, a motor-car treasure hunt, sports, a swimming gala, open-air dancing, in fact there was so much going on that it was almost impossible to see everything.

One high spot of the week's celebrations was the Soap Box Derby, organised in the market place. This, of course, was an event for the younger male element of the town, but I believe that some fathers put up a good show too!

The major event of the week was the grand Carnival Procession through the streets of the town, with fancy dress competitions for the children and adults, clowns, decorated cars and lorries, plenty of music from three bands and the whole impressive array led by the hounds of Puckeridge Hunt with the Master in hunting pink. The winning tableau was presented by St John Ambulance Brigade, and there is no doubt that this was the finest spectacle that has been seen in a local procession for many years.

After the distribution of the prizes, there was open-air dancing in the car park, Old Time dancing in the Town Hall and celebrations throughout Baldock until finally the week's revelries were brought to a close by a very impressive tattoo staged in the foreground of the Baldock factory. Singing was led by the Rector of Baldock, Canon L P Smith. The Chairman of the Council expressed his thanks to all helpers and stated that it was fitting that the finale of the week's celebrations should take place in the Kayser Bondor grounds, where Her Majesty the Queen, then Princess Elizabeth, had once been a visitor. The proceedings came to a close with the singing of a hymn and at the sounding of the Last Post – the standards were dipped.

A generation of children was growing up who had no memories of the war. Their battles took place in the playground — or in the classroom with their long-suffering teachers.

I went to Pond Lane School – but I didn't like it, and on my first day I got smacked – I think it was for crying because I didn't like it. I went home at dinner time, well, I think it was a little before dinner time and me mother had to take me back and I think it was when she disappeared that I got a rap over the knuckles with a ruler.

I got the slipper first day at Senior School, too. We were all

*The Coronation Pipe-Smoking
Contest. Only one match was
allowed to get the pipe going,
with two others for relighting
purposes, but both carried a
ten-minute penalty if used.*

*Two 'big-heads' in the
coronation procession cause
some consternation with the
younger members of the
crowd.*

The fancy dress line-up.

The winning team in the Ladies Coronation Football Match.

The Red Cross float passing along Hitchin Street.

Schoolchildren cheerfully showing off their coronation mugs on a chilly June day.

lined up and Mr Gregory came along and he said, 'What's your name?' So I told him and he said, 'Is Roy your brother?' and I said 'Yes'. Then he said, 'Bend over', and he slippered me and said, 'I owed him that from last year!' But he was a good teacher really.

In my second year at junior school, we had this teacher, Mr Brunty, and he was really keen on boxing and wanted to have a competition and asked for volunteers. Well, I don't remember volunteering, but I found myself matched against this big bloke – he was really tall and I was still quite small. And we had to box in the classroom itself and I remember the classroom had an old fireplace and I caught the opponent with a lucky punch and he fell into this fireplace. The second fight happened when I met my opponent in Mansfield Road. And we started fighting just because we were matched against each other the next day; I got a bloody nose and this was just the rehearsal! The real thing was to be in the playground, but I did a sly thing: for three rounds I back-peddled so he never actually laid a glove on me and I never laid a glove on him and I was declared the loser for being 'less aggressive'.

Nine o'clock on an early spring morning in the High Street c. 1960 showing rush-hour traffic!

I went to Weston Way Nursery school when I was about three. It was built as a temporary nursery but it is still standing. I was collected from there by Mrs Kingsley until Mum picked me up. During the day we had hot milk and toast soldiers then had to have a rest on a camp bed. I used to go and hide in the woods with a couple of mates 'cos I didn't like having a rest. I left there and went to St Mary's Infants' School. They did good dinners there. I then went to Pond Lane when I was about seven or eight. When I left Pond Lane I went to Park Street School in the top Juniors for about three years. My favourite teacher was Mrs Kline. When I was at Pond Lane and it rained there was a very deep puddle or so it seemed to us and we were always told not to go in it, but we always did.

On the way to Pond Lane School we would call in at Lucas's sweet shop on the corner of Church Street and Sun Street, then wander on down and go in what used to be a church down Pond Lane. There was an old boy who had a horse and cart selling fruit – near the paint factory – and we'd ask him if he had any old fruit and he'd give us a couple of apples to take to school.

Top: Children obviously enjoying themselves on the horse in the Avenue Park playground.
Middle: The class of '59. Children with teacher Ian Piper at St Mary's Junior School.
Bottom: Sports Day at Baldock Secondary Modern School (now Knights Templar). The long mound with hollyhocks growing on it was the school's wartime air-raid shelter.

When I went from Pond Lane to Park Street I got stood inside the fireguard for fighting with a new boy to the school. That was when I was in Mrs Dunn's class.

After there I went to Baldock Secondary Modern School. Mr Lennox was the headmaster. There was one teacher we didn't like, so one day we decided to get our own back and when he went to go home he found his bike in pieces! There were these huts at the back of the school and one day we went in there and piled all the desks and chairs in front of the door, then climbed out of the window and waited with the rest of the class at the front for the teacher. When the teacher came, he opened the door and sent all these desks and chairs flying.

We used to do cross country running which I didn't like so when we did the short run, we used to go up Farm Lane and while most of them went on round the top and back down Weston Way, a few of us used to nip into a friend's house for a cup of coffee, then meet the others as they came past the bottom of Chilvers Bank. When we did the long run which was up by the creamery we would sometimes get a lift back on a milk float.

Although caning was still practised when I was at school, I never got it, surprisingly.

When I was in the third year at school, they started the fifth year and there was only about four pupils in it. Most of the kids left at 15. When I reached the fifth year there were about 20 pupils staying on. You only took about 2 or 3 'O' levels and 'A' levels were unheard of. They probably did them in the Grammer School.

There were no clubs after school – it was straight in and straight out, you were out like greased lightening and you ran home to miss the posse of boys who wanted to give you a thump!

There were still two private schools here – Grove House, where the girls wore straw hats, and the convent school, which had been in Pepper Court and then moved to South Lodge. Many of the girls there were Greek Cypriots – their parents kept cafes and restaurants in London and they lived in the French Convent – the Sisters of Divine Providence – it was a French order so it was known as the French Convent. Some of the children were there from the age of three and there was a nursery class there. Working mothers would take their children there at seven or seven-thirty, they'd be given breakfast and dinner and collected again later.

Discipline was rigidly enforced during school hours, but once the bell went, the children, and the boys in particular, were just as much a nuisance to the local constabulary and fruit-growers as ever their fathers and grandfathers had been.

We went to Baldock Youth Club in the Secondary Modern School and, of course, Bysouth's yard was nearby. And going past the back of there one day, where the school tennis courts now are, me

and my friend Eric saw these Victoria plums in Bysouth's garden, so we nipped over the fence and stuffed all these plums down our jumpers. But the lady who was working there saw us and told Bysouth and he and his lad came out and chased us, and we legged it, with these plums shooting out of our pullovers all over the road. Bysouth and his lad would not give up the pursuit and I disappeared into the field where the Scout Hut is now and I lay down in the long grass there and I've never laid so flat in all my life – needless to say the plums had now all disappeared. Eventually he gave up, but I'm sure he knew it was us, but he never said anything. I got on well with him really. I had my sledge made there.

When it snowed we'd take our sledges up the Weston Hills and you could slide from the top of the hills there, right the way down past Woodlands Hostel. It was a long haul back up again but it was worth it.

There was a game keeper up Bush Wood who was quite a nice chap actually, we'd go over in the spring and pinch a few pheasants' eggs. And I can remember one time getting caught by him and usually he'd just give you a good talking to. But this time one of the lads had put his eggs under his hat – only two or three – and the old gamekeeper knew what we'd done but he didn't say anything. He just told us not to go over to Bush Wood again, then he said, 'Go on then, off you go,' and patted my friend hard on the head so all this egg yolk dripped down his face.

I was up there once with some friends and a boy called Tony and we weren't doing much – just looking for pheasants, when this pheasant flew up at the other side of what looked like a muddy puddle with a log across it, and we decided to go round and have a look. Well, Tony lost his footing and fell into this 'puddle' and, I'm not kidding, he went straight up to his neck – I thought he was going – but he managed to crawl out with a bit of help – he didn't smell too good and as soon as he was out, he was up on his feet and he was gone – we couldn't catch him and he ran all the way home from Bush Wood to Baldock.

I used to collect birds' eggs – we didn't know it was wrong then – and we'd always be up trees and in bushes scrabbling in the nests. Then I got this chest infection and had an X-ray and the doctor asked if I'd got any budgerigars. And my mother said, 'Well he's always up trees and round birds' nests and playing with birds' eggs.' The doctor said that could have caused it, so when we got home, my mother threw my whole collection on the fire – I said, 'That's all my life's work!'

We used to catch slow-worms and lizards – we'd catch them by their tails. They would bask in the sun on the bonnets of cars in the scrap yard and we'd put them in tobacco tins, and once I took one home and said, 'Mum, Mum, look at this.' There was this big

Three keen members of 1st Baldock Cubs.

scream and she shot out of the house and straight up the end of the garden. Quite wonderful it was!

When I was in the Scouts we were taken off for a whole day down to Hatfield or Hertford to what looked like an old bomb site. And there were Scouts from other troops there, too, and we had to queue up and be given labels to pin on ourselves which listed what our injuries were. Then we were given carte-blanche to go any-where – just spread ourselves out on this site, and after a while two blokes came along and read our labels and if you were 'dead' you were just left there, but if you had an injury a stretcher was brought up and you were 'attended' to. But we got a good meal there that day. I can't remember how we got there, but usually if we went to camp we'd get chucked in the back of Mr Moules' removal lorry – all the tents got thrown in the back and all the scouts got thrown in on top of them and we'd stay like that all the way up to West Runton.

I remember PC Wilkins – he was hard but fair – but everything I ever owned he confiscated; I had the first metal catapult in town. I hit this six-foot sign on the railway bridge – a direct hit – and he only happened to be standing behind me at the time, so he took that. And he confiscated me roller skates as well, because I constantly skated up and down that pavement outside Labrums –

Church Street with the old Eight Bells pub on the right.

that nice slope there, you could really get up a speed – and he warned me three times, so he took them away. But it was my catapult I really wanted back and he wouldn't give it to me.

I remember a bloke called Dave, who used to make 'certain suggestions' to the girls on the coaches going through to the hockey matches when they stopped in the High Street, and he got a real clout round the ear from the local bobby who happened to be walking past. They wouldn't dare do it now.

The thing was if I'd gone home and told me Dad that the local bobby had confiscated my skates or clipped me round the ear, he'd have given me another one. He was a good policeman though, because he knew all that was going on and he knew everybody.

I remember my Uncle Bill cycling from Letchworth and he came up the High Street and PC Wilkins said, 'Hello Bill – do you know your back light's not working?' 'Yes, I know,' says Uncle Bill, 'but I'm on my way home.' And he went on home up the High Street and down Pinnocks Lane. PC Wilkins cut through, went across the football field and caught him and fined him! and they'd just had this conversation – so he must have had second thoughts.

He was the sort of bloke you had to pit your wits against. If you wanted to go scrumping you had to know where PC Wilkins was before you ever set out.

Living close to the Weston Hills we spent most of our free time up there. We used to ride a three-wheeled bike down the Weston Road with wood as the front axle. Of course, the wood broke, we came off, so we replaced the piece of wood and carried on. We used to sledge down the Weston Hills, all the way down Woodland Way and onto the London Road. We'd sometimes make a train of about 14 sledges, the first one would crash and there would be a terrible mess everywhere. Before Chiltern Road was made up, we built a dam across the road when it rained. Someone would come up the road and drive through it so we would have to repair the dam. One year, when there was a lot of snow, we made a big snowball and rolled it down from the hills and were taking it to the back field in Chiltern Road. As we were going across the road a mate's dad's car was coming, so we left it there and he crashed into it. He knew it was us so he gave us a walloping.

With Mother working at the Bondor, most of the holidays were spent swimming in their pool.

We used to go scrumping, as all kids did, but we were not satisfied with taking a few apples, we'd strip a tree completely. A lady sat up in her bedroom watching us, followed us home, took all the apples back and we didn't 'alf get a walloping from the parents. One of my worst memories was having to come home from school in the winter to a dark, cold house especially when the meter had run out and we couldn't find two bob to put in it.

We used to spend weeks building a bonfire for Bonfire Night. We would try and build it as big as we could, always bigger than the previous year – the whole street turned out. There would be bonfire toffee. A couple of days afterwards we would go and put spuds in the embers and cook them. We'd go to Mrs Darts to buy fireworks – bangers of course.

A chilly, sunny day in the High Street with a Luton-bound double-decker waiting for its passengers c. 1960.

In the bad winter of early '63 everything had seized up and nothing was getting through and Dad made me get a trolley and we trudged all the way down to the station from Chilvers Bank in the snow; and all the coal wagons were in a siding there, nothing could be delivered you had to go down and get your own coal, and I remember the blokes opening up the wagon and this one big solid lump of coal coming out and we had to drag it all the way back on this trolley, with the wood of the trolley cracking under the weight.

I used to work on a butcher's van all day Saturday. I earned 7/6 for a 10-hour day, plus a bit of meat or a tin of fruit for my dinner. We used to sell cornish pasties at 8d each or three for 2/- and most people would take three even if there were only two in the family. I left school when I was 16 and went as an apprentice at Kryn and Lahy, Letchworth, until I was 21.

And still the fair was the highlight of the year. The confetti had disappeared, but it remained a magical time where you could meet old friends and perhaps win an amazing prize.

*Opposite: The glamour of the
Mysterious East — for adults
only — at Baldock Fair.
Bottom right: The younger
generation were more
interested in candy floss
anyway.*

The excitement of the fair was wonderful. As you got nearer you could hear the noise and when you turned the corner from Mansfield Road into the High Street it was wonderful with the lights, the music, the smells. And all down the road they used to park the trucks where they hung their equipment on great big hooks. On the way to school the most daring boys would hang onto these hooks and swing down on them.

And at night everything seemed so mysterious because you weren't usually allowed out after dark and you could hear a sound like a hum getting louder as you approached the fair, then it all hit you just as you turned the corner.

We had The Dodgems, Jollity Farm and The Whip and The Cakewalk – the Big Wheel came in later. They used to have things where the men could show off their strength. There was a big hammer and the men had to hit a metal surface in order to make a bell ring. All the girls would stand round and egg their boyfriends on to see who was strongest. I only had one go but I couldn't hit it hard enough to make the bell ring, so that was the first and last time I tried.

Then there was the punch ball that you pulled down and it was suspended on a chain. You had to hit it and see how far it made a needle swing round. This was another favourite with the young men who wanted to show their muscles off.

There was the ghost train too and the tunnel of love and if you were asked to go on that, well . . . but I don't know how good that was – I was never asked on!'

The prizes were all made of soft plaster or chalk and you could play hopscotch with them for weeks after. But you could also win china – my brother won a fruit set.

The first time I went to the fair on my own I won a canteen of cutlery on the Bingo. All the forks and spoons used to bend after a while.

Down Whitehorse Street there used to be Billy Woods' Boxing Booth, just near The Vic Pub, and most of the contenders came out of the pub. The usual sequence of events was that there would be five or six bouts in an evening and Billy Woods would put up his champion and anyone who was prepared to take on Billy Woods' fighter had to go three rounds and they could win a fiver.

I remember one chap from Stevenage was fighting Billy Woods' champion and there was a local referee who wasn't in a great state really and I think it got to Round 2 when, out of the blue, the Stevenage fighter catches the champion a heavy punch and knocks him to the canvas and we were all there cheering and in the excitement the crowd stamped and shouted and counted to 10 and so counted him out. But the referee, in his infinite wisdom,

says *he* was the referee and he would start the count when and where he thought fit to do so, and he couldn't count while we were making such a noise, so, of course, he started his count after the 10 and by about 15 or 16 the fair bloke got up and knocked seven bells out of the Stevenage man. So the poor Stevenage bloke never won his fight, but at the end of the event stalls and God knows what else went flying into the ring and, needless to say, the referee retired to the Vic and was never seen again.

The booth was very popular and, in fact, it was so popular that, after the fair had gone, it quite often stayed and moved, I believe, to the field behind St Joseph's Convent up by the motorway. And it would stay up there for a week or a fortnight – just as long as it was still taking money. It was always the local boys wanted to show off. But most of it was for real – there was quite a lot of blood there at times. It faded out about the mid-sixties.

It was held in a marquee and the champion would be paraded outside and they'd call out, 'Can you beat the Champion?' and, just like the films, the girls would look at their boyfriends and say, 'Go on, you can beat him.' But they didn't fancy their bloke any more when he came out covered in blood! But there were a few hard cases in the town who could well look after themselves.

The Bondor remained the major employer in the town, and in its paternalistic way provided for the children of the workers as well. It was always more than just a factory.

You could use the sports' facilities at the Bondor if your parents worked there – you'd be given a membership card. But you could always get in with friends. If you wanted to go swimming and had

Below: A new range of nylons being modelled in the Kayser Bondor magazine, Summer 1960. A survey showed that women thought stocking tops ugly but lingerie exciting, so these had coloured tops and were called 'Intrigue'!
Below right: A cartoon from Kayser Bondor magazine for November 1954.

"Well, you asked for a false front, old boy!"

a membership card it cost you 3d, but if you took a guest, they had to pay 6d or perhaps it was a shilling. And if you hadn't got a swimming costume they'd always got one they could lend you. Every year they'd give free membership to the first half-dozen in the pool when it re-opened in the spring. The water would be 40°F, but you'd strip off and hit the water and be out the other side so quick . . . but you'd get your free membership for the year.

All my family worked for the Kayser Bondor so I think the bloke on the gate thought I did too. I never payed a penny into their sports' fund and I never worked there, but I've played football for the Kayser Bondor and cricket, too. They had lovely tennis courts there and a beautiful bowling green.

The children of Bondor employees all had a Christmas treat. The very young ones had a party in the canteen and the older ones were taken to a pantomime in London. Before that, though, they used to get professionals in to put on a show for the children in the big old canteen there, but later they started to go to London.

The only time I worked for the Bondor was when I was in the Scouts. We worked all over the weekend – Saturday, Saturday night and Sunday. When they built the new warehouses near Holroyd Crescent they wanted to transfer all their stock from the factory to the new warehouses, so they did some sort of deal with the Scoutmaster and they had conveyor belts going from the old building right across the fields into the new buildings and we stayed up all night long – we thought it was great. We just had to

The swimming pool and fountain in the Kayser Bondor grounds on the High Street. The Astonia Cinema was directly opposite.

drag the stock off the shelves and put it on the conveyor belt.

The Bondor factory was in magnificent grounds and they had a groundsman, Mr Bonfield, who really used to care for it. The bowls green was superb – and there were two grass tennis courts and all the flower beds and shrubs were well-tended and the swimming pool was looked after. The main gates were never used except for special occasions but they opened onto a drive with great wide flower beds either side which always looked magnificent. And as you came up Pinnocks Lane towards the High Street you could see the waterfall effect of the fountain splashing into the swimming pool. There was a lovely house, too, in the corner of the grounds, near where Tesco's petrol pumps now are; it was originally the Managing Director's house and was later used for guests.

Television hadn't yet made an impact on the population as a whole, so people still looked outside the home for entertainment. Dances, fetes and bazaars were held regularly and the teenagers could always find something to do.

The Soap Box Derby was quite an event. John Gregson, the actor, came down for it one year and Giles, the cartoonist, often came and he drew a cartoon once for the Daily Express depicting Baldock's Soap Box Derby.

First of all, all the go-carts would line up and be judged for the most original design and there were some really good ideas. Then there would be heats, divided into two age groups, I think. And I remember one year the final was between two carts, one belonging to two boys called Dashwood and Chalkley and the other driven by two much bigger lads. So there was a staggered start to give the smaller lads a bit of a chance, but they weren't really expected to win. It was an exciting race, though, with Dashwood and Chalkley just winning it on the line. and their cart turned over and Barry Dashwood grazed his knee, but it was a great race.

There was an oval track marked out in the market place and this wasn't just a small event. I can remember hundreds of people being down there to watch it. Traffic was kept in line with straw bales. I imagine it took place during the six weeks' school holidays – there were lots of carts entered, with several heats before the final – it took all afternoon. I think it only ran for two or three years, but I don't know why it stopped. The West Ham speedway star, Fred Curtis, used to present the prizes – and a bike was quite a good prize.

The Cubs used to meet in the upstairs shed in the garden of Dr Riddell's, where the surgery used to be, then we moved to the upstairs of what is now the Tyre Depot, then to an Anderson Shelter up Hopewell Road. Then we moved to the British Legion

Hut behind the Congregational Church. Eventually the parents all got together and built the Scout Hut on the Park.

There were the annual Church Fetes that we used to go to, held in the Rectory garden. And there was some sort of fete or garden party held in Dr Riddell's garden in the High Street, it was a kind of tea party – the garden was beautiful there and there was a very old mulberry tree there in this lovely secret garden.

The Astonia was a favourite place to go. It was beautiful inside and upstairs it was one of the best cinemas in the area. It had double seats. It was the only cinema I've been in where you didn't have to stand up for people passing along the rows. There was plenty of space – very luxurious and downstairs there was also a

Budding Stirling Moss's lining up for the 'off' at the Soap Box Derby.

Cartoon of the Soap Box Derby drawn by Giles of the Daily Express.

café with a glass front – all very Art Deco. I was taken there on treat days – for a birthday or something like that.

Mr Ayres was the owner/manager and he always stood there in a nice suit and made sure there was no funny business – it's said his sister was Ruby M Ayres, the novelist.

I've been thrown out of the cinema many times for making a noise. I used to go to the cinema about three times a week and if I got banned for a week that was really terrible. There would be a change of programme on a Thursday night and then a different film would be shown on Sundays. There were different categories of cinema for 'A' circuit films and 'B' circuit and we were never on the 'A' circuit – we used to get 'B' films – Edgar Wallace and things like that, and I think Sunday must have been on a 'C' circuit!

We used to go to the Sunday night cinema and the Edgar Wallace film would be showing but we'd be playing pontoon!

There used to be a hall behind where the Heath Hall flats are now and they used to let it out for wedding receptions and things like that.

We used to go to the Summerhouse café up the Royston Road and they used to deal in American cigarettes and we'd go in there for our Lucky Strike and Passing Clouds. That was a right den of iniquity for us.

Another of my dens of iniquity – well it wasn't really, its just when we got in there it became one – was Baldock Social Club in the old church rooms in Whitehorse Street. It was pulled down a few years ago, but it used to stand almost opposite the Post Office. It used to have a big snooker table there and a table-tennis table and the people running it would come round and watch us,

Bottom right: The Astonia Cinema in the High Street — 'the most comfortable cinema in North Herts'.
Below: A week's programmes at The Astonia, 1965.

ASTONIA
BALDOCK
Tel. Baldock 3366

NOVEMBER 21-27

SUNDAY and MONDAY
Peter Cushing in
DR. TERROR'S HOUSE OF HORRORS
Sun. 5.0, 8.20; Mon. 5.30, 8.50 (X)
also HE RIDES TALL
Sun. 6.40; Mon. 7.10   (X)

TUESDAY and WEDNESDAY
Melina Mercouri and
Peter Ustinov in TOPKAPI
5.30, 8.10   (U)
FULL SUPPORTING
PROGRAMME 7.30

THURSDAY - SATURDAY
WHERE THE RIVER BENDS
5.45, 8.45   (U)
Abbott and Costello in
LOST IN ALASKA
7.15   (U)

but if you got there early there was a lovely card table in the corner and we used to play cards. It actually taught me a good lesson because I was an apprentice at the time and I'd only been at work for a few weeks and I used to bring home £1.18.4d a week and I used to give my mother £1 and I had 18/4d – well, this particular night I went down the Baldock Social Club and I lost it in a hand of Shoot Pontoon and I thought to myself it took me 45 hours to earn that and about five minutes to lose it. And I never gambled like that again.

The Stag at the bottom of Church Street was really ace – it was purely a domino place and you only went in there if you wanted to play 'Fives and threes'. It cost you half-a-crown to play. But it was just like a front room. It was the only pub without a bar, you were waited on. The barrel used to be on the table and it was in this little room just before you got to their living room. It wasn't a ladies pub – the only woman who went in there was Mrs Bullard and she was part of the furniture.

We used to go to Baldock Working Men's Club in the old building before it was pulled down. And we'd go to dances there, but you didn't have to dance to move around, the floorboards were so springy that when others were dancing, those standing round the edge watching went up and down as well. Me and Pete Williams used to go every Tuesday and Thursday nights because Pete's dad was on the door. We'd go to choir practice in the church and then out of choir practice and on the way back up Weston Way we'd call in and see Pete's dad. It was a brilliant place.

I went to the Clydesdale Dance Studios to learn to dance, but I didn't go for long because she kept partnering me with this girl who wore a leg iron and this girl was so much better at dancing than me that I gave up in disgust.

Members of the Baldock Youth Organisation performing two numbers from their very first show in 1966.

When I started at the Dance Studios I'd got a partner the same size as me, but I grew faster and when I finished there he still only came up to my chest! He was a nice little dancer but we had to part because he was so much smaller than me! They didn't have a studio – they used to hold their dance classes in the Town Hall and later on moved to the little church hall in Church Street.

We also had ballet classes in the British Legion hut which was behind Rusco's – now Pryor Court and Icknield Court – our teacher was a ballet dancer and had danced at the Windmill Theatre. She had ballet classes, stage classes, tap classes and she'd put on a show every year at the Town Hall – the Big Occasion. And afterwards everybody was presented with a bouquet of flowers and I remember thinking, 'I shan't get one, everybody's forgotten me', but my uncle had brought this little bouquet and gave it to me.

We spent hours in the back room of Allnutts Café 'til Freda came and chucked us out because we'd only had one cup of tea.

Baldock in the forties had a lot of very clever people living in it They had been brought to live locally to do research on radar at SERL and as well as working together they organised amazing 'themed' dances in their spare time. I can remember one dance where the Town Hall was transformed: it became a New Orleans river boat, complete with paddle wheel. The dances were often fancy dress and many a time we'd go to the George and Dragon for a drink beforehand and you could be in there rubbing shoulders with half a horse and a Cardinal . . .

I can remember going for a weekend away with my aunts and we used to catch the workmen's train in the morning, from Baldock Station. We were always late, my aunts got up late and then burnt the toast – we always had burnt toast – and we'd run up the road to the station, but there was always someone there who would hold the train for us and wait while we bought a ticket.

But if you did get there early, you'd go into the waiting room and there'd be a lovely fire there, and flowers and magazines on the polished table. And in the summer it was always ever so pretty with hanging baskets and an old barrow filled with flowers. They used to whitewash the stones that edged the flower-beds – it was really smart and clean, everything was polished.

The BYO (Baldock Youth Organisation) was formed in 1965 after a meeting of all the Church Youth Clubs and we decided we would get together and do something for the community. Its original aim was to help the residents of the town with gardening, decorating, painting, in fact, anything anybody wanted done. Then we decided to put on variety shows for the Senior Citizens. We performed these in Baldock Secondary Modern School. One of the jobs we did was to decorate the living room of one of the Alms-

houses. Even though I say it myself we did a good job. Unfortunately a few weeks later there was a fire there and all our hard work was ruined.

But the town was changing. The much-loved shops that had been here for decades, one by one, closed down. New towns were being built, more people owned cars and so out-of-town shopping became a weekend diversion. The world outside was beginning to impinge.

SERL (Services Electronic Reserch Laboratories) was one of the units built towards the end of the war in the hope that people would want to start using new factories. There were some very clever people working there but it seemed strange to me that just after the war they were developing guidance systems ready for another one. They experimented with lasers too. Up at Peartree Hill outside Baldock they built a gantry and they used to beam a laser down to a tower at the SERL factory.

It was all very secret there. So it was strange when the Russians, who worked at the UMO factory in Letchworth, came to live in the Hillcrest flats in the 60s, just the other side of Crabtree Lane to the SERL factory. Nobody who worked at the SERL could understand how the Ministry concerned could be so naïve as to let all these Russians come here – all their windows overlooked the SERL – they were the only houses or flats in the whole of Baldock that actually overlooked the SERL premises!

After the war, in the 1950s, the authorities were obsessed with the next one and the nuclear bomb; the WRVS were sent around to talk to women's groups – young wives, etc., telling them what to

Top: The Civil Defence Corps practising at the old Baldock Brewery in Pond Lane. Above: A Civil Defence volunteer with his vehicle decorated for the coronation procession.

do in the event of 'the bomb' being dropped. They hoped to reach one in five women with these talks but I think it worried more people than anything else because they were told they only had four minutes to get all the family together and get the pets out and sandbag the doors and the windows and fill the baths and dip the curtains in bicarbonate of soda. I can remember seeing a programme in the late 50s with Richard Dimbleby interviewing some people about this sort of thing and a good half of them said they thought it would be good idea if the heads of households were given a supply of suicide pills so that they could do away with the family!

When the Baldock bypass was built, as it was called then, that is the A1(M), which took all the traffic off the Great North Road, that's when Booths stores closed. Then a bit later Bishops, the ironmongers, who used to make all their own buckets and tin baths and things like that (well they did before the war anyway). Then a bit later again Pattersons closed, so by the late sixties all the big shops had gone.

I think several things caused that to happen. One was that more people had access to a car and then Stevenage New Town began to open up with the big chain stores. So for the first time ever, quite a lot of people could get out of the town to do their shopping and make a sort of outing of it. They also had more money to spend.

Mrs Bishop was almost the last of the Baldock ladies to keep a little shop of the old sort. Hers was about two doors down Church Street, she had a little counter where she'd got animal feed and goldfish and so on and then you could go into another little room for tea and sugar and general groceries, everything seemed to smell of soap and paraffin, because she sold that too. When her husband was alive they also had a zoo at Jaywick every summer. I certainly remember the salamanders and turtles and tortoises crawling around – that was on one side and you passed them to get to your food on the other side.

Then again, as people started to shop out of the town, which they hadn't been able to do before, people who had shops here wouldn't allow anybody else to open up in the town. So it pulled both ways, people shopped out of town for the greater variety of shops, whilst the shop keepers here were afraid of losing even more trade if they allowed more variety and choice in. In that way they prevented the variety of shops from being in the town, which was one of the reasons why people had started to shop elsewhere in the first place. They were able to do this because so many of them owned various properties throughout the town. You can understand why they decided to do that, but really it was the wrong decision.

When I was a kid I used to think, 'Why can't I live in a *proper* town with a Woolworths!'

And then the last brewery in the town, Simpson's, ceased production. For decades it had provided employment for successive generations and its demolition, three years after closure, signalled the end of an era.

My father said the brewery should have been kept for its brickwork alone. 'Look at that,' he said, 'What a beautiful bit of 18th century brickwork.' Now, of course, it would have been preserved. Ten years after its demolition, Greene King themselves said that they should have kept it as a brewery, but there, it all happened at just the wrong time.

I was talking to someone who used to do a bit of work for Simpson's Brewery just before it closed down and he said he had seen a scheme and drawings for the brewery to be turned into a shopping complex. They were going to keep the frontage and have an entrance there and all the old buildings were going to be turned into a shopping arcade.

Walking down The Twitchell from Baker's Close to the British Legion hut we used to see the hops in the field. There was a great big mountain of them. One day the brewery was all boarded up, then it just seemed to disappear.

Simpson's Brewery: closed 1965, demolished 1968.

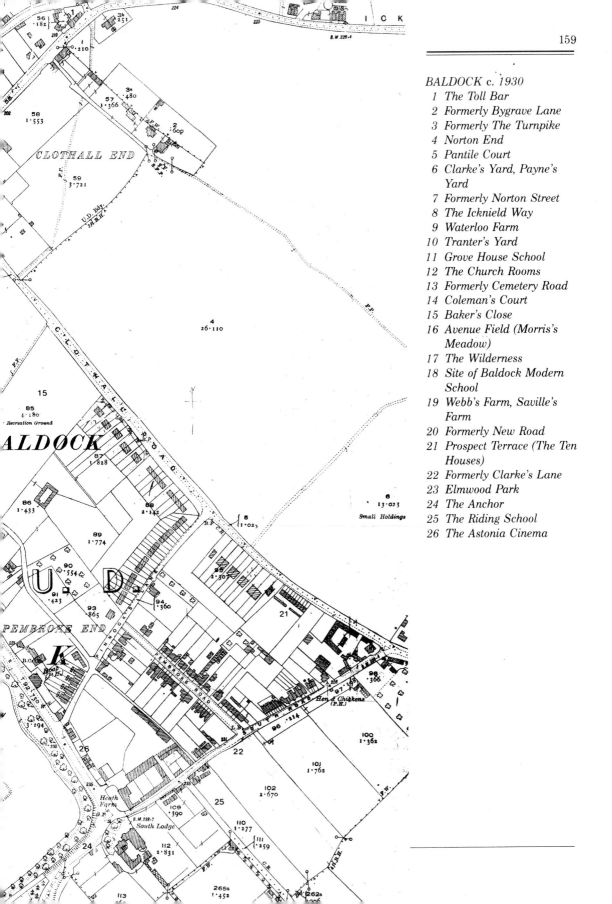

BALDOCK c. 1930
1 The Toll Bar
2 Formerly Bygrave Lane
3 Formerly The Turnpike
4 Norton End
5 Pantile Court
6 Clarke's Yard, Payne's
  Yard
7 Formerly Norton Street
8 The Icknield Way
9 Waterloo Farm
10 Tranter's Yard
11 Grove House School
12 The Church Rooms
13 Formerly Cemetery Road
14 Coleman's Court
15 Baker's Close
16 Avenue Field (Morris's
   Meadow)
17 The Wilderness
18 Site of Baldock Modern
   School
19 Webb's Farm, Saville's
   Farm
20 Formerly New Road
21 Prospect Terrace (The Ten
   Houses)
22 Formerly Clarke's Lane
23 Elmwood Park
24 The Anchor
25 The Riding School
26 The Astonia Cinema

Appendix

cock'orny   Possibly from cockernony meaning a coiffure or pad of false hair.

The Cross   Baldock Cross where the four main streets — High Street, Hitchin Street, Church Street and Whitehorse Street — meet.

Felix eyes   Striped sweets, like cats' eyes. Felix the cat was the first popular cartoon figure from the era of the silent films.

gleaning   Picking up fallen ears of grain after the corn has been reaped and taken from the field on the hay wagon. Often used as, or sold for, chicken feed to supplement the family's income.

locust beans   Carob beans which, when processed, provide a chocolate substitute.

maltster   Person who makes malt i.e. barley or other grain which is soaked in water, then allowed to sprout, and is finally dried.

Reckitt's Blue   A powder used in laundering to keep the clothes white.

The 'Passion Wagon'   Because so many servicemen were stationed in the area, efforts were made to keep them entertained. Lorries, or 'passion wagons' as they were known, would be sent into the town to transport local girls to dances on the outlying US camps. The girls were even chaperoned in the early days.

shock   stook or propped-up sheaves of corn.

twitchell   A narrow winding path between two high walls or hedges.

vinegar flats   large round 'pennies' of toffee.

white hearthstone   A soft chalky stone used for whitening hearths, doorsteps etc. It would be dampened and rubbed over hearth or step.

The Wilderness, Hitchin Street   The House was built in 1737 and was once owned by Thomas Pryor, squire of Weston. In the early 1900s the Morris family bought it, but the garden had been unattended for a while and was very overgrown. Local children played there and it became known as 'The Wilderness' because of the state of the garden. The name would appear to have stuck.

Average Wages:

Pre-World War I	£1 10s 0d (£1.50)
1920s/30s	£2 – £4
1940s	£5
1960s/70	£10 – £20

'Old money'

4 farthings (¼d)	= 1 penny (1d)
12 pennies	= 1 shilling (1s)
half-a-crown	= 2s 6d
20 shillings	= £1 0s 0d

Decimalisation was introduced in 1971.

1 new penny (1p)	= 2.4d (2.4 old pennies)
10p	= 2s 0d (two shillings)
100p	= £1

So, dress material in the 1940s which sold at 4½d a yard would have been slightly less than 2p. (1 yard = .914 metres.)